RUDOLPH KENNA

The Glasgow pub companion

ANGELS' SHARE®

NEIL WILSON PUBLISHING · GLASGOW · SCOTLAND

The Angels' Share is an imprint of
Neil Wilson Publishing Ltd
303a The Pentagon Centre
36 Washington Street
GLASGOW
G3 8AZ

Tel: 0141-221-1117
Fax: 0141-221-5363
E-mail: info@nwp.sol.co.uk
www.nwp.co.uk

A catalogue record for this book is available from the British Library.

ISBN 1-903238-00-5

Design and photography by Robbie Porteous
Printed in Spain

CONTENTS

CONTENTS

Merchant City

East End

South Side

North Side

INTRODUCTION

THE PRESENT-DAY Glasgow pub has its origins in the taverns of earlier centuries – modest private houses with liquor licences. Inns were much grander: the travel termini of their day. Frequently, Glasgow's old taverns were situated in closes, and sometimes even up flights of turnpike stairs. At their best they were snug parlours, where firelight played over sturdy furniture, china ornaments, copper utensils, and the quart pewter flagons known as 'tappit hens' – the name was a corruption of the French word 'topynet'. In 1690 puritanical civic leaders issued a proclamation against 'debauchery', banning drinking in taverns after 10pm on week nights, 'or in tyme of sermon, or therafter, on the Sabbath dayes'. The following year the authorities, on account of midnight disturbances, prohibited citizens from going 'through the toun in the night tyme maskerading, or sirenading, or in companie with viollis or other instruments of musick in any numbers'. The town's 17th century taverns served a wide selection of liquors. Ordinary folk drank ale (at that time a sweet-tasting drink, brewed without hops). The well-to-do were partial to a mixture of hot water and 'sack' – the ancestor of sherry. Claret from Bordeaux was also consumed by the town's wealthier citizens.

By the mid-18th century almost every hostelry had its conspicuous hanging sign, but in 1772 the civic authorities wanted these removed 'as they interrupt the views along the streets, and darken the light of the lamps in the night time'.

In the 18th century, drinking customs permeated all ranks of society. When an apprentice became a journeyman, celebratory drinks were in order. Merchants and shopkeepers took a 'meridian' or noon drink (often accompanied by a salt herring). Business agreements were sealed with a stoup of liquor. Religious debates took place over tankards of ale or tumblers of Glenlivet whisky, and lawyers met clients in convenient hostelries (the clients were expected to pay for the drinks).

Even cons were allowed a wee swally – in the 1790s the jailer at Glasgow's Tolbooth prison kept a taproom and purveyed porter and small beer to inmates. Different social classes patronised different taverns. No shopkeeper or tradesman would have had the effrontery to request a 'meridian' in a tavern frequented by men of rank.

Old Glasgow's congested nature made taverns a social necessity: all but the seriously rich lived in tenement flats, with no room to entertain. This changed in the Victorian era, when the upper middle class moved into spacious town houses and suburban villas. Magnificent purpose-built clubs offered luxurious facilities not available in the old taverns and refined society began to look down on pubs, which now drew customers mainly from the working and lower middle classes.

An 18th-century pub crawl was a hazardous experience. Public footpaths were rutted semi-middens. As late as 1780, city magistrates had to rebuke citizens for emptying chamber pots from windows in the time-honoured 'gardyloo' (gardez l'eau) manner. Robberies and assaults were common. In 1764, Glasgow was 'infected with a gang of villains, who, under cloud of night, attack people in the streets, carrying off hats, cloaks, or anything they can lay hold of'. When there was no moonlight, citizens used 'bouets' or hand-lamps. Nine primitive street lamps were installed in the Trongate in 1780, but were speedily vandalised. 'Policing' the town was the responsibility of a night guard drawn from the ranks of prosperous citizens between the ages of 16 and 60. Using the session-house of the Tron Kirk as their headquarters, they patrolled wynds and streets from 10pm until about 4am. After that, the town was unguarded. Though a primitive law-enforcement agency by modern standards, Glasgow's 18th-century 'police' did manage to clock up a few arrests. In 1781 a young man, 'disordered in his mind by intemperane', got nicked for vandalising the equestrian statue of William of Orange – at that time the principle ornament of Trongate.

Customs and Habits

Until the mid-18th century, one of the favourite beverages was 'tippenny' ale, which cost 2d a Scotch pint (equivalent to an English quart). Glasgow Punch was the chief drink at assemblies and supper parties. Served cold, it consisted of one-third Jamaica rum to two-thirds water, flavoured to taste with sugar, nutmeg, and the juices of limes and lemons. In the early 18th century,

Glaswegians were also fond of a peculiar local brew called herb ale. It appears to have been made from malt, the dried leaves of ground ivy or alehoof, and dried roots of tuberous bitter vetch. These ingredients were boiled together, without hops, and fermented with barm. According to another traditional recipe, herb ale was produced by steeping juniper, wormwood, watercress, dandelion roots and orange peel in beer wort. In the early 1890s, The Old Herb House, famous for its herb ale, still stood at the corner of Green Street and Great Hamilton Street, east of Glasgow Cross.

By the late 1700s, porter – a dark, heavy-bodied, bitter-tasting beer, originally sold in London – was brewed locally by Murdoch, Warroch and Company, at their Anderston Brewery, and also by John Struthers, whose brewery was situated in Calton. Since Glaswegians had a penchant for sweet-tasting ale, porter was a great novelty.

In the early 1800s, some Glasgow taverns had bowling greens and skittle alleys. In 1823, The Nottingham Tavern, in Dunlop Street, had a 'new billiard table, equal, if not superior, to any in town'. Pressure of space in the rapidly expanding Victorian city and the rise of punctilious licensing authorities, hostile to pub games and amusements, conspired to remove such amenities. To their credit, the authorities also banned cruel diversions such as cock-fighting and 'drawing the badger', in which a badger was lodged in a barrel and the 'sport' consisted of setting a dog on the unfortunate creature.

Old Glasgow clubs used the city's taverns as meeting places. The Grog Club met in The Black Boy Tavern, Gallowgate. At club meetings, grog – diluted navy rum – was circulated round the table in a large wooden 'quaigh'. In the 1780s, some Highland gentlemen residing in Glasgow established a Gaelic Club, which met in Mrs Scheid's tavern in Buchanan's Court, off Trongate. Members were obliged to wear 'tartan short-coats'. Anyone failing to do so was fined a bottle of rum. Every Saturday, members of the Anderston Club, an association of wits and savants founded by Dr Robert Simson, a celebrated mathematician, left the city and walked to the then country village of Anderston, via the villages of Grahamston and Brownfield. Their destination was a tavern belonging to John Sharpe, 'ane god-fearing host'. Members included printers Robert and Andrew Foulis and Adam Smith, author of *The Wealth of Nations*. Sharpe's tavern – at that time the only hostelry in Anderston – served 'howtowdie' (hen broth), followed by saddle of mutton, washed down with Medoc and punch.

Every morning, members of the Morning and Evening Club collected newspapers from the Post Office, then adjourned to a comfortable tavern in Currie's Close, on the east side of High Street, to absorb the latest 'intelligence' from London over tankards of hot herb ale or 'baurie' (rum toddy). Club members met again in the evening, when they drank considerable quantities of 'mahogany' – mulled port wine. The Garrick Club, largely drawn from the theatrical profession, met in McLaren's Tavern, opposite the Theatre Royal in Dunlop Street. Habitués also included artists such as John Mossman and Sam Bough. The City Club (later, the Burns Club) met in The Bank Tavern, Trongate, and comprised leading literary men of the town, including Hugh Macdonald, Robert Buchanan, and William Miller.

Every night, at 7.45pm, the Tron steeple bell warned people with letters to post that the receiving box for south-bound mail was about to close. At the sound of the bell, a mercantile fraternity, known as the Post Office Club, met in John Neilson's tavern, in Tontine Close, to gossip over rum toddy.

Life in Georgian Glasgow wasn't all strong drink and frivolity, however, and citizens could be deeply serious. According to an 18th-century guidebook: ' . . . in going out of doors in an evening, you may hear so many singing psalms, that strangers are apt to imagine themselves in church'.

In the early 1800s, the Banditti Club, an association of affluent young ruffians, met in Gardner's Tavern in Gibson's Wynd, where they drank until midnight. They then roamed the streets, playing practical jokes. Their favourite prank was 'boxing a Charlie' – tumbling over a night watchman's sentry box, so that the elderly occupant was trapped underneath. At that period, every twelfth house in Glasgow was reckoned to be a tavern of sorts. One visitor walked from the foot of Saltmarket to the top of High Street and counted 80 places of refreshment. Perhaps he was seeing double by the time he got to the top of the street. By 1850, there were 2,000 licensed premises in Glasgow – one for every 160 citizens.

As early as the 18th century, Glaswegians were suffering from terrible hangovers. In 1760, 'Dr Ratcliff's Purging Elixer' claimed to 'cleanse the body of all cross and vicious humours, contracted by heavy drinking'. As an added bonus, the Elixer also cured smallpox, scrofula, deafness, scurvy, and dropsy.

By the end of the 18th century, some Glasgow taverns had become centres for radical activity. In the 1790s, The Thackit Hoose, Main Street, Gorbals, was a meeting place for supporters of the French Revolution. In 1820, soldiers arrested 27 Radical Society delegates 'in full conclave' at a Gallowgate tavern. Sympathisers pelted the troops with stones and 'brick bats'.

In the early 19th century, The Institution in King Street, near Glasgow Cross, patronised by Sir Walter Scott, was much frequented by students and professors from the University, at that time located in High Street. Patrons travelled considerable distances to savour The Institution's old-fashioned atmosphere, eat collops or 'brandered' (grilled) steak, and drink ale or stout from antique silver tankards. By the end of the century, lawyers and journalists attending the High Court were among the old tavern's habitués. Author and journalist Neil Munro – creator of Para Handy – recalled lunching there 'on a slice of silverside and a flagon of ale in company with junior members of the Scottish bar.'

In the 1850s, adherents of pugilism met in The Zebra Tavern, located in Zebra Close (40 High Street), kept by John Goldie, ex-prize fighter and local hero. Goldie later transferred his business to The Pugilist's Howff in Seaton's Close, off Saltmarket. Pugilism crossed class barriers. The Pugilist's Howff was patronised by the Duke of Hamilton, Lord Kelburne, and the latter's strange protégé, Rab Ha' (Robert Hall), the famous 'Glesca glutton'. The Olive, at 178 Trongate, stocked 'London and Scotch Porters', along with Edinburgh and Alloa ales, and London and Scottish daily papers. The stamp tax on newspapers wasn't repealed until 1855 so only the well-heeled could afford them. The poor made do with cheaply-printed sensational broadsheets, hawked through the town.

Hero-worshipping Victorians named many of their taverns after famous statesmen, soldiers and poets. The Lord Byron, in Jamaica Street, attracted a large seafaring element from ships in the Broomielaw. The Lord Clyde in Brunswick Street, supposedly one of the first places in Glasgow where India Pale Ale was sold, served beer in mugs decorated with a portrait of Sir Colin

Campbell (aka Lord Clyde), veteran of Lucknow and the Crimea. In late-Victorian Trongate, The Rabbie Burns Vaults was a shrine to the national bard: the pub's stained-glass windows were decorated with scenes from his works. In Gallowgate, General Wolfe's Inn had a more tangible link with the great and good: Wolfe was billeted there in 1749-50, when it was Camlachie Mansion.

The Victorian mania for bric-a-brac was also reflected in pub decor. Taverns such as The Waverley in Old Wynd, leading off Trongate, housed 'curiosities' such as stuffed animals, old weapons, and skeletons. The St Rollox Tavern in Castle Street was a veritable curiosity shop, its sitting-room walls hung with historic paintings and engravings. Pub 'museums' went back a long way. There was a Museum Tavern in Anderston as early as 1815; the landlord, Thomas Stevenson, stuffed birds, beasts and reptiles as a sideline. In late-Victorian times, Glasgow bar owners usually bought their conversation pieces from Hunter's curio warehouse in Argyle Street, which stocked everything from silver-mounted bagpipes to stuffed Russian bears. One of the last Glasgow pubs to exhibit dodgy 'museum' specimens was The Mally Arms in Eglinton Street. As late as the 1980s, the eccentric bric-a-brac included a stuffed crocodile. The Uisge Beatha in Woodlands Road has kept up the tradition to the present day.

In the 1840s, The Boar's Head Inn, in Marshall Street, near Gallowgate Barracks, was patronised by soldiers of the 71st Infantry regiment, known as 'The Glasgow Keelies'. At a critical stage in the Battle Of Vittoria (1813), against the French in northern Spain, Colonel Cadogan allegedly spurred his troops on by waving his hat and crying: 'Chase them down the Gallowgate!' The Aquatic Tavern in Trongate wasn't a haven for water drinkers, but was owned by Duncan Campbell, Scotland's champion sculler.

By mid-century, gin palaces were prevalent in Glasgow. They were a new type of urban pub, primarily designed for quick service and 'perpendicular drinking' at counters. Their garish exteriors were lit by huge gas lamps. Interiors were fitted with polished mahogany counters, tall mirrors, and gilded vats. When the city's first gin palace was opened in Trongate, in 1855, it was an instant success and police were needed to control the crowds jostling to obtain entry. The varying qualities of gin were known as 'Old Tom' and 'Young Tom' – a reference to the distiller's trade mark, which depicted a tom cat perched on a barrel.

Midnight Scenes and Social Photographs by 'Shadow' (1858), an early example of investigative journalism, refers to pubs with 'flaring gas lights in frosted globes, and brightly gilded spirit casks'. Despite brilliant illumination and meretricious ornament, gin palaces were sordid places, clustering in the poorest districts. But they were a strong influence on the 'palace pubs' of the 1880s, which adopted their mirrors, long bars, and rows of spirit casks

Glasgow's late-Victorian pubs differed considerably from pubs south of the border, which were usually divided up into class-conscious 'private bar/saloon bar/public bar' drinking areas. In Glasgow, most pubs consisted of a single democratic drinking space – of which The Horse Shoe Bar in Drury Street, now well into its second century, is the finest surviving example.

People's Palaces

The remarkable flowering of decorative arts in 1890s Glasgow was reflected in pub decor. There were many flamboyant pubs near the city's numerous theatres and music halls. Some had show business connections.

The Comedy Bar, at the junction of Bath Street and Buchanan Street, was a gallery of music hall celebrities. George Peat's Pavilion Bar was in Hope Street, at the heart of Glasgow's 'theatreland'. A special favourite with the 'artistes', it displayed copies of *The Era* and *The Stage*. The Rob Roy stood almost opposite the Royal Princess's Theatre (now the Citizen's) in Main Street, Gorbals, and boasted a series of decorative paintings and stained-glass windows depicting scenes from the life of the Highland outlaw. The Old Hampden Café in Bridge Street, frequented by pantomime stars from the Royal Princess's, was also popular with footballers and cricketers. The owner, J.G. Crichton, was a member of Queen's Park Football Club. Crichton's establishment, celebrated for oyster suppers, was one of the most handsome pubs in fin-de-siècle Glasgow. Its walls were hung with valuable paintings and engravings, along with curios such as Japanese swords and Gurkha knives.

Despite rich decor, Victorian pubs had sawdust on their floors.

Pipe-smoking or tobacco-chewing patrons didn't always take the trouble to use spittoons provided by the management. To boost trade, bar owners installed musical novelties such as the Polyphon. This ancestor of the juke box, operated by a penny-in-the-slot mechanism, played 12 popular melodies. In the early 1900s, some enterprising Glasgow publicans installed electric lights, a great novelty at the time, when most pubs and private dwellings were illuminated by gaslight. As late as 1901, Glasgow had fewer than 3,000 domestic consumers of electricity.

In 1901, Graham's Bar at Glasgow Cross, famous for its giant hanging lamp, was remodelled in just 36 hours by builders Hutcheson and Grant. These transformations were facilitated by the ready availability of materials such as anaglypta and lincrusta: easy-to-apply embossed papers, giving realistic imitations of hand-modelled plasterwork and similar labour-intensive forms of decoration.

In the 1900s, pubs helped pioneer the avant-garde 'Glasgow Style', but most were swept away before the style's importance was widely recognised. The St Mungo Vintner's (9 Queen Street), an outstanding example of Glasgow art nouveau, with extravagant joinery, rich stained glass and pictorial tiled panels by the great Doulton designer John McLennan, was shipped to the USA in 1974.

How old is the oldest pub?

Many pubs claim to be 'the oldest in Glasgow'. Usually, this means there has been a hostelry on or near the same site (not necessarily the same pub in the same building) for a very long time. In architectural terms, Glasgow's oldest pubs only date from the 19th century. Just over a century ago, however, pubs such as The Institution in King Street, The Old Eagle Inn in Maxwell Street, The Old Burnt Barns in Calton, and The Old Hundred Acre Inn at Port Dundas, could genuinely lay claim to long pedigrees. From the 1870s, Glasgow's oldest inns and taverns were destroyed by the City Improvement Trust, which obliterated the old town's labyrinthine wynds and closes. The Dove Inn, on the west side of High Street, was a typical casualty of progress. It was demolished in 1900. A stone from this historic inn, dated 1595, is preserved in the People's Palace Museum.

In the 1890s and early 1900s, magistrates waged war on the city's few remaining old-fashioned caravanserais. Glasgow bailies, imbued with temperance sentiments, disapproved of pubs, but were prepared to tolerate them as 'a necessary evil' – if they were modernised to facilitate 'overall supervision' by bar staff. The last historic taverns were torn down and replaced by open-plan pubs, with island bars. The magistrates declared themselves well-satisfied with the transformation. By 1914, there were hundreds of island bars in Glasgow. One of the finest examples has survived in The Horse Shoe in Drury Street.

In the early 1890s, the Corporation of Glasgow owned more than 30 pubs, obtained, along with a number of slum properties, under the City Improvement Acts. The Corporation let some of these pubs from year to year, but, gradually, licences were withdrawn as the city fathers demolished condemned buildings and replaced them with 'model tenements'. At the peak of temperance influence, the Trustees refused to allow pubs in new Improvement Trust tenements. Their successors in the Corporation Housing Department followed suit. The 'high heid yins' didn't relent until the 1960s, when they at last permitted pubs in vast peripheral housing estates such as Drumchapel and Easterhouse. There's still a dearth of pubs in these districts, each the size of Perth.

When a half was not a half

Victorian Glasgow had a large admixture of Highland and Irish newcomers, so whisky rapidly became the pre-eminent spirit in public houses. In the 19th century, whisky merchants began to mix traditional pot-still whisky with patent-still grain spirit to produce light blends which could be sold worldwide. Entrepreneurs such as James Buchanan and Thomas Dewar made fortunes from blended whiskies, but many obscure Glasgow publicans also made up their own special blends. Gantries, with rows of polished whisky casks, became prominent features in most pubs. Sold from barrels, Victorian public house whisky varied between 110 proof and 80 proof. Many publicans 'specials' were crude mixtures rather than carefully balanced blends of malt and grain. They sold for sixpence per gill. Bottled proprietary whiskies cost as little as 2s 6d, although better brands cost up to four shillings (20p) per bottle. Until 1915, no legislation existed to compel spirit merchants to mature alcohol for a minimum period before sale. Adulteration was common. An 1870s examination of whiskies in Glasgow pubs revealed an 'Islay whisky' containing meths and turpentine. Other adulterants included shellac, potato spirit, sulphate of copper, apple brandy, sulphuric acid, and wood alcohol.

Cheap adulterated whisky, known as 'kill-the-carter', possessed stupifying and inflammatory properties, especially when taken on an empty stomach. High Street, Bridgegate, Saltmarket and Gallowgate were notoriously drunken and rowdy on Saturday nights. Visitors claimed they'd never seen so many reeling drunks. Until the 1920s, police used a 'drunk's barrow', a long narrow hand-barrow fitted with a stretcher – to which the prostrate inebriate was firmly attached, by means of leather straps. It's now in Strathclyde Police Museum.

With so much bad whisky in circulation, drinkers would have been wise to stick to beer. Even that called for caution. In the late 19th-century, ales with an original gravity of 1160 were quite common. McEwan's 126 Shilling sweet ale and William Younger's Twelve Guinea Ale were just two of a very large number of potent brews. Around 1900, Edinburgh had 36 breweries. Glasgow, where water was suitable for brewing stout rather than pale ale, had 14. Edinburgh, Alloa, and English beers were popular in late-Victorian Glasgow. Citizens also managed to down pints from local brewers such as Gillespie and Sons (Crown Brewery), Steel and Coulson (Greenhead Brewery), and William Adamson (Barrowfield Brewery). Lager was just coming into fashion in the Edwardian period. Connoisseurs drank genuine draught Bavarian Spaten-brau, sold in the Panorama Restaurant, in Sauchiehall Street. Patriots could stick to Scottish lagers, brewed (under German supervision) by Tennent of Glasgow and Jeffrey of Edinburgh.

Huge amounts of beer were consumed in some pubs. In 1891, Glasgow publican Alexander Stewart purchased a complete March brewing of McEwan's 90 Shilling ale – 125 hogsheads (55-gallon barrels). In the late 1890s, a 'schooner of beer' was a popular and affordable refreshment in Glasgow. Tumblers known as 'schooners' held 2d worth of beer – two-thirds of an Imperial pint (bitter beer cost 3d per pint).

As early as 1889, a contributor to *The Victualling Trades' Review* complained that Scots seldom got a full glass of beer, since it was usually topped up with a large head of foam. He compared this unhappy state of affairs with Munich, where owners of beer halls were legally obliged to fill each oversize mug or glass until the fluid beer reached the litre or half-litre mark. More than a century later, Scots are still waiting for a similar square deal.

In late-Victorian Glasgow, many pubs installed new beer dispensing systems, based on hydraulic compression – a combination of air and water pressure. Compact engines converted mains water pressure into air pressure, which then pushed beer from cellars to service points. Bar staff filled glasses by opening taps, not pulling handles, as in the case of traditional hand-pumps. Water engines also raised whisky and other spirits from pub cellars to barrels on gantries. Archibald Bruce, a Glasgow plumber, pioneered 'Bruce, Challenge and Waste Not' water engines. In 1892, *The Victualling Trades' Review* observed that in Glasgow, his engines were 'almost in universal use'. Allan and Bogle and McGlashan water engines were also manufactured in Glasgow. A century later, the wheel has turned full circle, and most of the city's 'real ale' pubs use hand-pumps to dispense their ales. In Victorian times, counter fonts were invariably placed below the level of bar tops – an arrangement which allowed unscrupulous publicans to use 'slops' or waste beer without fear of detection. Tall fonts – requiring glasses to be filled above counters and in full view of customers – were a much later innovation. They were still in use in a few traditional Glasgow pubs at the beginning of the 21st century.

In 1903, Glasgow's licensing magistrates banned barmaids – to save them from 'a fate worse than death'. Concern arose because the city's pubs were overwhelmingly male-orientated. Women of the demimonde drank in the low dram shops of Bridgegate and Gallowgate, and a handful of upmarket pubs in middle class districts admitted 'respectable' women, but as a rule Glasgow women steered clear of pubs. The convention of men-only pubs baffled English and Continental visitors. Larger Edwardian pubs employed a host of barmen – uniformly garbed in long white aprons and white shirts. In the early 1900s, an average Glasgow barman worked a 65-hour week, and magistrates recommended a maximum working week of 60 hours.

Temperance

As early as 1829, a total abstinence society was launched in Maryhill. In the ensuing decades, Scotland's temperance movement mounted militant anti-drink campaigns, securing such important victories as the Home Drummond Act (1828) and the Forbes Mackenzie Act (1853). Undoubtedly the drink trade required regulation. In 1828, a tavernkeeper in Saltmarket was fined £5 for selling whisky to four young lads, one of whom was carried unconscious to the police office. The Forbes Mackenzie Act, which closed Scotland's pubs at 11pm on weekdays and all day on Sundays, gave new opportunities to individuals living on the edge of Victorian society. In 1855, Hannah McConvill was fined £7 for keeping a shebeen in Dog's Close, Calton. By 1857, it was reckoned that there were over 400 shebeens in Glasgow. Closes in the old town were honeycombed with shebeens, and there were also considerable numbers of peripatetic shebeeners who hawked their wares around the streets. The city's shebeeners usually obtained their whisky from illicit distillers. In 1862, John Lynch was fined £12 10/- for keeping an illegal spirit still in his house at World's End, Finnieston. In 1871, 250 shebeeners were convicted and 450 people arrested for drinking in shebeens.

Some temperance zealots tended to ignore the manifold causes of poverty, claiming that people were poor simply because they drank. In 1892, at a mass meeting of unemployed in George Square, Bailie Samuel Chisholm, who attributed all the ills of society to 'the drink traffic', was branded a 'canting, humbugging, hypocritical liar'. Operating on the dubious principle that sobriety could banish poverty, Glasgow Corporation established an institution for 'pauper inebriates', housing them in Girgenti, a mansion house in Ayrshire. In 1907 the staff reported that attempts to cure the inmates by means of drugs had met with failure. At that time Girgenti accommodated 130 indigent alcoholics of both sexes. Private enterprise provided similar facilities for alcoholics from prosperous backgrounds. In the early 1900s, the Hagey Institute, established in Glasgow in 1898, offered to cure 'alcoholic diseases' in 'three weeks only'. The Institute stressed: 'All communications strictly confidential'.

The temperance movement's campaigning zeal led to the Temperance (Scotland) Act of 1913, which allowed each parish, burgh or ward to decide by vote whether to keep all the pubs, close all the pubs, or – the third option – close some of the pubs. The first so-called 'Local Veto Polls' were held in the early 1920s, and resulted in the demise of a number of Glasgow pubs, including George Farmer's handsome Edwardian establishment at Parkhead Cross. The pub became a branch of the Clydesdale Bank. Veto Polls were abolished in 1976. 'Local Veto' enthusiasts would have been horrified if they could have looked into the future, for by the end of the 20th century, many Glasgow banks had been turned into pubs. The ratepayers of Parkhead had voted for the 'limitation' of licences, but in other areas, including Cathcart and Whiteinch, residents voted for local prohibition. During the First World War, restrictions and shortages put a temporary stop to heavy drinking in Glasgow. The Defence of the Realm Act (DORA) curtailed opening hours. Between 1914 and 1920, duty on whisky rose from 14s 9d per proof gallon to 72s 6d. In the 1920s, comedian Will Fyffe lamented that whisky was 'twelve an' a tanner a bottle' (62p).

Changing style

Many Victorian and Edwardian pubs survived until the 1930s, when owners began to revamp their premises in art deco and art moderne styles. New pubs had exteriors of brightly coloured vitrolite (a fashionable glass cladding). They also featured peach-mirrored walls, indirect lighting sources and exotic wood veneers. Lounge bars exploded outworn taboos and admitted women. Patrons showed their sophistication by asking for cocktails – *The Savoy Cocktail Book*, published in 1930, gave recipes for more than 700 varieties. In 1937, the teetotal Band of Hope warned Glaswegians: 'The cocktail habit is slowly enmeshing the young womanhood of the country. To the less stable mind its social appeal is not the least of its dangerous attractions.' Pubs from the stylish 'cocktail era' have all but vanished – one of the last to be 'improved' out of existence was the vitrolite-fronted Thornwood Bar, in Partick. Three outstanding examples can still be enjoyed – The Rogano, The Steps Bar and The Portland Arms.

Some remarkable pubs survived into the inter-war period. Dirty Dick's was situated in the heart of dockland, in Finnieston Street, near the original Clyde Tunnel. The pub drew its customers from every corner of the globe. Every day, staff went to the bank with a bag of foreign currency. Coins such as francs, marks and South African half crowns were regularly tendered and accepted. A rupee was worth 1s 4d at Dirty Dick's.

By the 1960s, most traditional Glasgow pubs had been replaced by bars with wall-to-wall carpets and decor ranging from mediocre to execrable. Ironically, the lost pubs represented superb Scottish craftsmanship in woodcarving, glass staining and embossing. Young people were being enticed into naff 'theme' pubs such as The Kimberley Queen, Tollcross Road ('the realistic surroundings of an old man o' war') or The Tyrol, Argyle Street ('the atmosphere of a Tyrolean inn'). Mock-Tudor pubs also took off in the 1960s – though there had been a previous 'Tudor' vogue in the interwar period. In the 1960s, the style was characterised by half-timbered interiors, horse brasses, copper warming pans and female staff in nylon tabards. The Doublet, Park Road, is the finest surviving example of the genre.

Hundreds of pubs were destroyed during Glasgow's comprehensive development programme, which ripped the hearts out of communities such as Townhead, Anderston and Springburn. With few exceptions, no attempts were made to salvage magnificent bar fittings and advertising mirrors. However, Ruxton's Bar, at 21 Elderslie Street, Anderston, was carefully dismantled and transported to the USA, where it was used as a film set for westerns.

In the 1980s, heritage became a commodity, marketed for mass consumption. With Glasgow giddily aspiring to post-industrial *ville lumiére* status, the period also saw the rehabilitation of many listed buildings. But the city's few remaining historic pubs still didn't enjoy adequate statutory protection. In the late 1990s, The Corona (1912-13) at Shawlands Cross, the finest early 20th century pub in Glasgow, was torn apart by its corporate owners, who relaunched it as a link in a new – and inevitably transient – 'branded pub chain'. In the same period, the city lost two outstanding examples of 'Glasgow Style' pub design, dating respectively from 1900 and 1904. It's likely that, in the near future, many more traditional pubs will be targeted in this manner, and will lose their individuality in the process.

While historic pubs have fared badly, Glasgow's burgeoning leisure sector has come to the aid of much of the city's threatened built heritage such as banks, fire stations, churches, cinemas, and even schools. Listed buildings given a new lease of life in the 1990s as 'superpubs' included Langside Free Church; the Bank of Scotland, St Vincent Place; the Phoenix Assurance building, St Vincent Street; Woodlands Public School, and Lanarkshire House, Ingram Street. In Anniesland, a derelict art deco office block was transformed into a pub, restaurant and micro-brewery. It's too early to measure the effect of these heavily capitalised 'superpubs' on the traditional pub culture of Glasgow. By the end of the 20th century, Glasgow was also home to lots of trendy 'style' bars – a phenomenon which will almost certainly prove as ephemeral as previous theme bar fashions. Overtly gay bars emerged in the 1970s. One of the earliest such pubs in the city was The Waterloo Bar, Argyle Street. The city now has a lively gay pub scene – including at least one lesbians-only bar.

Live music and culinary variety are comparatively new additions to Glasgow's pub scene. Victorian licensing magistrates disapproved of singing in pubs, and it was not until the 1960s that, with relaxation of old Calvinist standards, live folk music became a major attraction in pubs such as The Victoria Bar and The Scotia. One of the most popular folk songs of this period paid tribute to the convivial atmosphere in a typical working class pub – Quin's Bar in Springburn (since demolished):

Doon in the wee room, underneath the sterr
Everybody's happy, everybody's therr.

Pub grub

In Georgian times, Glasgow's taverns offered a wide range of delicacies, including red herrings, known as 'Glasgow magistrates' – the term derived from the red gowns worn by the city's bailies. Beefsteaks of heroic proportions were served up in Bryce Davidson's tavern, Stockwell Street (then the home of many wealthy merchants). Salmon – readily obtained from the River Clyde – would also have been in plentiful supply in the town's inns and taverns. In 1864 The Pope's Eye Tavern, Argyle Street, offered 'hotch potch' and 'dressed tripe' at 6d per portion. Another pub in the same street advertised 'beef steak, 4d, Allsopp or Bass, 1d per half pint, wine, 2d per glass'.

To discourage drinking on empty stomachs, late-Victorian licensing authorities insisted that pubs provide food as well as drink. Favourite pub snacks of the period included welsh rarebit, steak and kidneys on toast, oatcakes and cheese, and herring and potatoes. In the 1890s, customers of The Old Hampden Café consumed three or four barrels of oysters every week. By the 1960s, Glasgow pub fare usually consisted of mutton pies, sometimes garnished with peas or beans. Now, many city pubs provide appetising meals and snacks, from traditional Scottish delicacies to cosmopolitan cuisine.

The variety of drinks vended in Glasgow pubs has never been greater. Vodka has overtaken blended whisky as the favourite 'short'. While there has been a sharp fall in blended whisky consumption, Scotland is witnessing an upswing in demand for single malt whiskies. Most sensible bar-owners stock a wide choice of malts; the most enterprising have gantries crammed with several hundred single malts and de luxe blends. In the mid-1990s, industry bosses launched a stylish campaign of TV commercials to promote whisky as a trendy drink, but travel has broadened the horizons of ordinary people, and 'the cratur' now faces stiff competition from drinks imported from around the globe.

Lager now outsells all other beers, and consumers can seek out premium brews from Europe, North and South America, Africa, Australia, the Caribbean, and the Far East. Low-alcohol drinks are widely available, though these are not a novelty: in the 1890s Tonbur (Burton with the syllables reversed) non-intoxicating 'beer' was brewed in Glasgow at the former Clydesdale Brewery in Victoria Road.

Time, gentlemen, please

Opening hours are more liberal than at any time since the early 19th century. In 1904, Glasgow adopted closing at 10pm. In the 1920s, the city's pubs closed at 9.30pm and although 10pm closing was reintroduced in 1932, Captain Percy Sillitoe, the hard-nosed Chief Constable of the day, insisted that customers leave licensed premises promptly on the hour. The Licensing (Scotland) Act of 1976 extended evening hours and introduced Sunday and all-day opening.

When sexual discrimination became illegal, in 1975, the all-male Glasgow pub culture, extolled in Hugh MacDairmid's essay *The Dour Drinkers of Glasgow*, became untenable. It had been losing ground since the 1950s, when MacDairmid grumpily dismissed unisex pubs as 'deScotticised resorts' and boasted that he preferred 'a complete absence of women on occasions of libation'. Children's certificates were introduced in 1991, but licensing boards can set stringent conditions before issuing such certificates, including the installation of special low-level children's sinks and toilets, thermostatically controlled tap water, covered electric sockets, and removal of gambling machines and pool tables.

Real ale

Cask-conditioned ale accounts for only a tiny fraction of Scottish beer sales, but there is, nevertheless, more real ale available in Glasgow today than at any time since the 1960s. But large areas of the city – the east end and the peripheral housing estates – remain 'real ale deserts' with little hope of improvement. Most real ale pubs are concentrated in the city centre and the west end. Some free houses offer a wide range of real ales, along with rotating selections of guest beers. Even pubs tied to breweries offer wide and changing ranges of cask beers. And several city pubs now operate micro-breweries and offer real ales brewed on the premises. We owe this happy situation to the Campaign for Real Ale (CAMRA). Cask ale is not pasteurised, like keg beer. Yeast is still active when the ale arrives at a pub and a secondary fermentation occurs *in situ*. Keg beer is effectively sterile – all living organisms have been killed off, and extraneous gas is added prior to serving.

CAMRA has made clear its opposition to sophisticated 'mixed gas' keg technology which simulates the smooth character of genuine cask-conditioned ales. Mixed gas products are more palatable than their fizzy predecessors, but they are not real ales. To confuse the unwary, they are sometimes dispensed via fake handpumps or tall fonts, traditionally associated with real ales.

INTRODUCTION

While some famous Glasgow pubs have altered little in 80, 90 or 100 years, most modern pubs are unlikely to acquire that degree of permanency. In today's rapidly changing milieu, pubs regularly undergo refurbishment. They all-too-frequently change their names. The pub scene can alter very quickly in response to trends – as in the mid-1990s spread of 'Irish' theme bars and the current wave of 'style' bars and 'superpubs' in listed buildings. In the interval between writing and publication, some of the hostelries featured in this new edition of *The Glasgow Pub Companion* will probably change their names and characters. I hope the changes will be for the better. And once again I apologize in advance if they are not.

Rudolph Kenna, 2001

Note: Some of the pubs listed in *The Glasgow Pub Companion* have ex-directory telephone numbers.

The M8 (incorporating the north and west flanks of the Inner Ring Road) effectively cuts central Glasgow in half, with the city centre east of the M8 and the west end west of the motorway. The damage inflicted on the city's townscape by this 'engineering triumph' of the 1970s is painfully visible at Charing Cross, where the urban motorway removed the Grand Hotel, isolated the Mitchell Library, and divided world-famous Sauchiehall Street into 'eastern' and 'western' sections.

A century ago, pubs were a rarity in the exclusive residential west end: in 1898, working class Calton had 120 pubs and only four licensed grocers, while middle-class Kelvinside had 14 licensed grocers and only one pub. Now there are pubs in the west end to suit every taste, from old pubs of character to trendy café-bars.

The jewel in the west end's crown is the Park Conservation Area, a hilly faubourg, representative of Victorian town planning at its most confident, and dominated by the three Lombardic towers of Charles Wilson's Trinity College, now converted into flats and offices. The magnificent townscape is worth exploring on foot – and there are several excellent watering holes in the vicinity. The Park Conservation Area's finest town house – 22 Park Circus – is now Glasgow's 'Palace of Weddings'.

The **Aragon**

131 Byres Road, G12,
0141 339 3252

Popular student-friendly hostelry, with a hanging sign depicting a monk hard at work in a monastic scriptorium. The University

of Glasgow, where undergraduates famously pursue their studies with contempt for worldly pursuits, is a short distance from here. Pubs such as The Aragon are modelled on rustic hostelries in obscure corners of rural England rather than on the flamboyant and superbly urban 'palace pubs' of late Victorian Glasgow. With low ceilings, bare wooden floors, redundant barrels and nicotine yellow walls, they are the thematic equivalents of earlier mock-Tudor pub trends. Cheap snacks and good selection of regular and guest real ales.

The **Attic**

44-46 Ashton Lane, G12
0141 334 6688

Attractive bijou hostelry, situated above the long-established Cul de Sac pub and restaurant. Features a central, open raftered roof and waist level fire. Handy for cosmopolitan Byres Road and the University quarter. Brunch is served here, and the inexpensive tapas menu is worth sampling. There's also a good selection of wines.

The **Avalon**

25 Kent Road, G3
0141 564 1263

Originally called Barrie's Vaults after its Victorian

landlord. A friendly unpretentious bar/lounge situated opposite the Mitchell Library, The Avalon offers a good selection of inexpensive bar lunches and live music at weekends.

Bar **Bola**

144 Park Road, G4
0141 339 2992

Now a trendy 'style bar' with Iberian-inspired mosaics, comfy sofas and intimate booths, this was formerly The Blythswood Cottage, a typical mock-Tudor pub of the 1960s. But *plus ca change*, and the present establishment is as popular with students and locals as was its predecessor. Varied menu includes Mexican, Thai and Mediterranean dishes. Sunday brunch served from noon until 8pm. Drink promos most nights.

Bar **Brel**

39-43 Ashton Lane, G12
0141 342 4966

Popular café-bar located in a former stable in one of the West End's most trendy locales. Offers exceptional variety of imported beers. Food served all day, with special deals between 5pm and 7pm.

Bar **Oz**

499 Great Western Road, G12
0141 334 0884

Formerly Chimmy Chungas, a bar/cantina, located in Cooper's Building, a famous Victorian grocery establishment. The circular clock tower (1886) is a conspicious west end feature visible from some way down Great Western Road. The entrance is flanked by pillars of polished granite, and the

vestibule is paved with colourful tiles. Now one of a chain of Antipodean theme bars, with tabletops in the shape of surfboards and a DJ's box disguised as a lifeguard tower. Popular with students, who, in legendary Australian fashion, down four-pint pitchers of the 'amber nectar'. Bar fare includes burgers and pasta dishes. Satellite and cable coverage of major sporting events. DJ Fri/Sat.

Bar **Stazione**

1051 Gt. Western Road, G12
0141 576 7576

In the mid-1890s a fashionable Glasgow architect, J J Burnet, designed the Lanarkshire and Dumbartonshire Railway's Kelvingrove station to look like a typical west end villa residence, so that the station didn't stand out like a sore thumb and cause deep distress to the well-heeled locals. All the best people lived in villas along this stretch of Great Western Road. The former station, located at the entrance to Gartnavel General Hospital, now houses the Stazione bar and restaurant, offering a pleasant traditional ambience and well-prepared snacks and meals.

Bar **Zoo**

80 Dumbarton Road, G11
0141 334 8012

Formerly known as Reid's of Pertyck and The Western Tavern, this pub was owned in Edwardian times by Thomas C Reid, a kenspeckle figure in the local community (he was chairman of Partick

Thistle FC) The original monumental bar fittings have gone, but there survives from Reid's ebullient era a fine ceiling carried on cast-iron pillars with ornate capitals. Food served Mon-Wed 12-7; Thur-Sat 12-9; Sun 12.30-9. Drink promos Sun-Tue-Thur 7-11; Fri 4-7.

The **Ben Nevis**

1147 Argyle Street, G3
0141 576 5204

Refurbishment (1999) of a long-established Argyle Street local with strong Highland associations. The new Ben Nevis is a cosy pub with a Scottish vernacular theme. Well-run and user-friendly, it's within easy walking distance of Kelvingrove Art Galleries. Drinks are reasonably priced, and there's an excellent range of malt whiskies. Live Traditional Scottish music every other Thursday night.

Argyle Street has always had strong links with the Gaelic world. In *The Brave Days*, Neil Munro wrote: 'We came to "Glasgow of the

Steeples" from the hills, expecting from generations of Gaelic tradition to find Argyle Street the most amazing thoroughfare in Scotland, and we were not disappointed.'

Big Blue Bar

445 Great Western Road, G12
0141 357 1038

Pleasant Mediterranean-style café-bar, located in an old railway arch. Weather permitting, traditional Italian dishes can be enjoyed alfresco on a terrace overlooking the river Kelvin (not the Arno or the Adige, but never mind). The Big Blue sells many varieties of grappa. Produced in the Veneto, especially in the town of Bassano del Grappa, this favourite tipple of Venice's gondoliers is consumed unaged and white, or aged in oak barrels, where it takes on a rich, amber shade. In 1601, the Doge of Venice created a University Confraternity of Aqua Vitae to control the quality of grappa.

The **Bon Accord**

151 North Street, G3
0141 248 4427

This famous hostelry celebrated its 21st birthday in 1995. A previous owner reputedly hailed from Aberdeen, the City of Bon Accord. Under new ownership some years back, the Bon

Accord acquired a split-level interior, a neo-Victorian long bar and gantry, and distressed plasterwork, so typical of 'ye olde' 1990s. As this book goes to press, the Bon Accord has changed hands and plans are afoot to revamp the pub. Well-kept range of rotating real ales. Good value meals and snacks.

Bonham's Wine Bar

192 Byres Road, G12
0141 357 3424

An attractive bistro on the site of the original foyer of the Grosvenor Picture House, which formerly had its main entrance in Byres Road. Bijou galleried interior, with two bars/buffets on separate levels. The decor consists of mirrors, marble-topped tables, ornamental cast-iron balustrades, and modern stained glass. Traditional pub menu served 12 noon-6pm. Snacks until closing time.

The Carnarvon Bar

129 St George's Road

This is the sort of no-frills Glesca 'drink shoap' associated with Hugh MacDiarmid's cantankerous essay *The Dour Drinkers of Glasgow*. A largely unspoilt Edwardian interior, with snugs, island bar and central gantry. Cast-iron pillars support a coffered ceiling. As for the habitués, they're actually far from dour. No Welsh associations here, the pub takes its name from its location – at the corner of Carnarvon Street.

The Canal

300 Bearsden Road, G13
0141 954 5333

American-style micro-brewery, bar and diner, opened in 1998 and trading as the Miller's Thumb Brewery Co. This welcome addition to the sparse amenities of the Temple district occupies a 1930s *art moderne* office block, all that survives from the once extensive Temple Saw Mills, founded in 1874 by Robertson, Dunn & Co. Six tasty ales, brewed on the premises, are on tap, and the micro-brewery can be viewed through plate glass. The decor is informal and a good choice of meals and snacks can be had in the attractive diner. The mainly young locals take the pervasive music and wide-screen TV in their stride, but more fastidious patrons can escape (weather permitting) to the rooftop beer garden overlooking the Forth and Clyde canal. Car park.

Cottier's

93 Hyndland Street, G11
0141 357 5827

Candlelit bar/restaurant, situated in the hall of former Dowanhill United Presbyterian Church, which now accommodates a small innovative theatre. The upstairs restaurant offers cosmopolitan fare. The place takes its name from Daniel Cottier, who designed the superb stained-glass windows in the church, built in 1865-66 by William Leiper, one of Glasgow's most famous Victorian architects.

Cul de Sac

44 Ashton Lane, G12
0141 334 8899

Popular, sparsely decorated bar/restaurant located at the end of a picturesque cobbled mews lane behind trendy Byres Road. Good café-bar atmosphere. Ground-floor creperie serves a varied lunch menu from 12 noon until 3 pm Mon-Sat. Sunday brunch noon until 4pm. Lunches are also served upstairs in the cosier Attic bar (see entry).

Curlers

256 Byres Road, G12
0141 338 6511

Originally, this was The Curler's Tavern, a historic link with old Hillhead. In 1900, when the clientele consisted of douce citizens of the independent burgh, the speciality of the house was Matthew D'Arcy & Co.'s Irish

whiskey, served straight from the wood. The pub, housed in an 18th century two-storey stone building, is now a fun palace for the area's student population, with bars on two levels, and pool tables, arcade machines and table football to take the punters' minds off Decartes and Wittgenstein.

Basic snack menu served during the day. DJs Wed, Fri-Sat. Local bands Tue.

Until the 1830s, when Great Western Road was laid down, Byres Road only went as far north as the present public library, before veering west towards Kirklee. In 1848, Partick Curling Club, formed in 1842, leased about an acre of ground for a curling pond opposite the present howff. After several years, the Club removed to a pond on the west side of Peel Street.

The Doublet

74 Park Road, G4
0141 334 1982

This friendly local, a short walk from Kelvinbridge Underground station, is an exceptionally well-preserved example of 1960s mock-Tudor, with fake beams and horse brasses. Naff at the

time, the genre has acquired scarcity value, and this pub, product of a more innocent age, is a gem. There's a cosy public bar here, with a lounge bar, overlooking the river Kelvin, upstairs. One of the city's oldest real ale outlets. Good range of whiskies stocked in the public bar. Food served all day. Satellite TV.

Dr Thirsty's Alehouse

65 Old Dumbarton Road, G3
0141 576 0203

Until 1993, this friendly unpretentious local was known as The Overflow (for The Stirling Castle opposite; see entry). The present name alludes to the close proximity of Yorkhill Hospital.

Until the late 1790s, when a new road to Dumbarton was formed, travellers between Glasgow and Partick passed The Bun and Yill House, a much-frequented tavern ('yill' is old Scots for 'ale'). This famous hostelry, dating from 1695, was demolished in 1849.

The Ettrick Bar

317 Dumbarton Road, G11
0141 576 0130

This well-frequented local was formerly The Criterion Bar, but there were two previous Ettrick Bars in Partick. The smaller of the two was situated in Castlebank Street, while its larger namesake, an art nouveau 'Glasgow Style' pub, was located at the corner of Crawford Street and Dumbarton Road. The present pub is a Victorian/Edwardian pastiche, with a long bar and gantry, leaded and bevelled glass, prints and knick-knacks. Inexpensive bar lunches are served in the well-appointed back saloon.

The **Exchequer**

56-61 Dumbarton Road, G11
0141 339 5741

Known for decades as The Roost, this pub, directly opposite the Western Infirmary, later became The Exchequer. By the late 1990s it had been transformed into one of the Firkin chain of branded real ale houses. The reversion to The Exchequer is all too typical of the arbitrary way in which Glasgow pubs now change their names. Though spacious and friendly, The Exchequer has little discernible character. Food is served throughout the day until 9pm. Sunday lunch available from 12.30pm.

Handy for the Museum of Transport and Kelvingrove Museum and Art Galleries, The Exchequer is not without distinguished antecedants. It was originally commissioned by Philip MacSorley in 1899 and completed the following year. Designed by James Hoey Craigie of Clarke and Bell, it was a typical 'Glasgow Style' pub, with an exuberantly carved wooden frontage (since incorporated in the present, much larger pub exterior). Two entrances led to a low-ceilinged public bar

with bench seating, a long bar, and a highly original art nouveau timber gantry. Craigie's original art nouveau public bar survived until the late 1990s.

The Scottish Brewing Archive is housed at 13 Thurso Street, a short walk from this pub. Annually, on the Archive's Open Day, some wonderful Scottish brewery memorabilia goes on display. For details of the event, contact the Archive (0141 339 8855).

Firebird

1321 Argyle Street, G3
0141 334 0594

Minimalist glass-fronted café-bar, offering an appetising menu and a good selection of wines. Handy for Kelvingrove Museum and Art Galleries. Happy hours Mon-Fri, 5-7pm. DJs throughout the week.

The **Grove**

8 Kelvingrove Street, G3
0141 221 8835

In the early 1890s, this no-frills Finnieston local was called The Tower Bar. Several years later a new owner, James Thomson, a Shetlander, renamed it The Flugga Bar, after Flugga Point. The pub evolved from ornate late-Victorian to comparatively uninteresting 1980s lounge bar style, via the art deco period. Note the nostalgic stained-glass door panel, reminiscent of idealised pictures in 1930s 'Metroland' brochures. Drinks cheaper than average. Bar snacks such as freshly cut sandwiches available all day. Friendly and witty regulars.

A few yards away, at 1125 Argyle Street, there's a two-storey ashlar-fronted building, dwarfed by neighbouring tenements. It was formerly The Sandyford Inn, used by travellers journeying along the main highway between Dumbarton and Glasgow.

The **Halt Bar**

160 Woodlands Road, G3
0141 564 1527

Named after one of the city's former tramway halts, this pub retains much Edwardian character. The unspoilt public bar boasts a large U-shaped counter, wooden dado, and lincrusta-style wallpaper. There's a wood-panelled snug at the rear and a fine Forrest and Son mirror, advertising Archibald Campbell's Edinburgh ales. Live bands perform twice weekly in the adjoining entertainment lounge, a modern addition. The Halt was a leading real ale pub of the 1980s and 90s, but sadly, cask ales are no longer available here. Fortunately there are two real ale pubs in the immediate vicinity! The Halt does, however, offer a good selection of single malts. Inexpensive bar snacks, noon until 5pm. Live music Wednesdays and Saturdays.

The Halt Bar stands opposite a bronze sculpture depicting Lobey Dosser, Sheriff of Calton Creek, and Rank Bajin, resident villain, riding tandem on Lobey's faithful two-legged friend, El Fideldo – products of Glasgow cartoonist Bud Neill's surrealistic imagination. Erected in 1992, the sculpture cost £18,000 – raised largely by public subscription. According to Bud Neill, Calton Creek, Arizona, was founded by punters from the Calton district of Glasgow's east end.

The **Hayburn Vaults**

429 Dumbarton Road, G11

This hostelry was designed by George Bell in 1904 for spirit merchants Robert Anderson & Co. A friendly and frequently bustling traditional Partick local, it has a handsome sub-art nouveau frontage and a large centrally-placed island bar. Inevitably, The Hayburn Vaults has suffered from 'improvements' and would

formerly have been a much grander pub. Partick didn't become part of Glasgow until 1912, but the local magistrates, as with their Glasgow counterparts, favoured open-planned pubs. Resourceful architects such as Bell, working within a confident decorative tradition, still managed to introduce character in the form of etched and brilliant-cut glass and similar refinements.

Karaoke evenings Tues, Fri, Sat.

The Hay Burn was a stream running down into old Partick. As late as 1850, what is now Hayburn Street was a country lane leading to a small dairy farm.

Hogshead

315 Woodlands Road, G3
0141 337 1790

This hostelry, the Scottish flagship of Whitbread's Hogshead Ale House pub chain, opened in 1999, and is located in the former Woodlands Public School, built in 1882 by Robert Dalglish for the Glasgow School Board. Most of the schools built in Glasgow in the wake of the enlightened

Education (Scotland) Act of 1873 were imposing buildings, and Jacobean-style Woodlands was no exception. The spacious pub, welcoming and unostentatious, has been fitted into the old school hall – part of which, with grand staircase, top-lit gallery, and decorative ironwork – is on view behind a timber and glass screen. In addition to a choice selection of traditional cask ales, and tasty meals and snacks, The Hogshead also offers a selection of premium bottled beers from around the world.

Hubbard's

508 Great Western Road, G12
0141 334 2995

This was originally a shop and restaurant, designed in 1929 for Hillhead baker Walter Hubbard. Note the faience-clad art deco upper storey. Now a large split-level pub in bogus vernacular style with wooden dados, sanded floorboards and artificially smoked walls, covered in old prints and photographs. Good selection of regular and guest real ales and reasonably priced meals and snacks.

The Islay Inn

1256 Argyle Street, G3
0141 334 1055

Formerly The Carousel Bar and The Outside Inn, this protean hostelry later became Fats O'Mally's, an 'Irish' theme pub. It then had a

short interval as a Welsh theme pub, and is now a Scottish theme pub! In the 1980s, as The Outside Inn, it was one of the pioneering real ale pubs in the city. Now a nondescript bar/diner in which real ales are conspicuous by their absence. Good selection of malts. Food available 12 noon until 9pm. Live music, pool and big screen TV.

JD Simpson's

1397 Argyle Street, G3

Formerly known as The Calypso Bar, this became a

Hogshead branded real ale pub in the mid-1990s. The Hogshead-style decor, including simulated oil lamps and redundant hogsheads (55-gallon barrels) has been retained and real ales are still available, though not in such abundance as in the Hogshead era. Inexpensive bar food. Daily drinks promos. Live music Thur-Sat.

This pub is directly opposite Kelvingrove Museum and Art Galleries, which emerged from the 1888 International Exhibition, when six million visitors (including Queen Victoria) came to Kelvingrove Park to view bibles in 200 languages, telegraph cables, and a 13-dial 'clock of all nations'. An architectural competition was held in 1891, and the foundation stone of the new Galleries laid in 1897. The building was completed in time for the even more successful International Exhibition of 1901. The Edwardian city fathers, many of whom were staunch teetotallers, were very keen on 'rational recreation' which, they believed, would provide counter-attractions to pubs and reduce the consumption of strong drink.

Jed Bar

239 North Street, G3

0141 204 1616

The Star Wars movies have cult followings as this theme bar shows. The atmosphere is relaxed and friendly and if aliens are encountered, they will doubtlessly be in a good mood. Lunches served 12-3pm. Food available throughout the day until closing time. Happy hours 5pm-8pm. Live bands. May the force be with you if you stay here all night (2 am Fri-Sun).

Jinty McGuinty's

23 Ashton Lane, G12
0141 339 0747

Highly-popular Irish bar located in former mews cottages/stables behind Byres Road, hub of the west end. Convenient for Hillhead Underground. Traditional decor with wood-panelled walls, embellished with portraits of Hibernian literary giants and quotations from their works. Bar food, including Irish specialities, served daily. Open Mon-Sat 11am-midnight; Sun 12.30pm-midnight. Beer garden.

The Lismore

206 Dumbarton Road, G11
0141 576 0102

Opened in the mid-1990s, this handsome Partick local compares very favourably with contemporary 'branded pub chain outlets' which are virtually identical the length and breadth of the UK. There are two bars here, a main bar with an attractive range of stained glass windows, and a small and cosy back bar.

The excellent pictorial windows – one of which depicts the Broomielaw and

good ship *Waverley*, the world's last sea-going paddle-steamer – show that lessons have been absorbed from the 'golden age' of the 1890s when stained glass was used widely in pub design, and pub windows glowed with colourful representations of sportsmen, inventors, poets, statesmen, monarchs, explorers, and soldiers.

Well-kept real ales and live fiddle sessions.

The Living Room

5-9 Byres Road, G12
0141 339 8511

Friendly and unusual bijou café-bar, popular with young trendies. The inventive kitsch decor includes a dry stane dyke bar and the finest flock wallpaper in Glasgow. Varied and moderately-priced lunch menu. DJs seven nights a week. Happy hours 5-8pm daily.

In the early 19th century, this part of Byres Road consisted of six small thatched cottages – three on either side of the road. In former times, the road was the route between Partick – an ancient village built around mills near the mouth of the river Kelvin – and the clachan of the Byres of Partick, where successive bishops of Glasgow are supposed to have kept their cattle.

Lock 27

1100 Crow Road, G13
0141 958 0853

Popular pub/diner at Lock 27 on the Forth and Clyde Canal, Anniesland. Decor includes lava lamps, leather sofas and a double-sided fish tank. Good value bar menu. With its own beer garden and child-friendly facilities, Lock 27 is a particularly attractive summer venue for families.

The Forth and Clyde Canal, linking the Firth of Forth and the Firth of Clyde, was reopened in May 2001, after decades of closure. In the 1840s, five passenger boats left Glasgow for Edinburgh every weekday, supplemented by three night boats known as 'hoolets' (owls). These leisurely voyages were popular with honeymoon couples. However, the opening, in 1842, of the

Edinburgh and Glasgow Railway dealt a severe blow to Forth and Clyde navigation.

A considerable number of horse-drawn pleasure craft continued to make use of the waterway and in 1866, the first screw steamer was introduced. In the 1900s two single screw steamers – *Fairy Queen* and *Gypsy Queen* plied daily from Port Dundas to Craigmarloch, a few miles beyond Kirkintilloch.

Moloco

287 Argyle Street, G3
0141 334 1550

Formerly Murphy's Pakora Bar, now a tapas bar which offers a variety of cuisine. Regular drinks promos. Live music sessions. Originally a Victorian pub called The Temple Bar – presumably a reference to the Temple of Solomon, since the distinctive 'Glasgow Style' building in Haugh Road, now a Muslim mission, was formerly Masonic Lodge St Vincent Sandyford No. 553. Many Victorian bar-owners were enthusiastic Freemasons and, disdaining secrecy, were happy to feature in the licensed trade press in full regalia.

The **New Arlington**

130 Woodlands Road, G3
0141 332 2128

A friendly local, near Charing Cross, with a multi-ethnic clientele, this basic lounge bar, formerly The Arlington Bar, was a pioneering Glasgow real ale pub in the early 1980s, serving Maclay's 70/- ale from antique McGlashan fonts. The current well-kept cask-conditioned ales are dispensed via handpumps. Good selection of malt whiskies plus bargain Malt of the Month. Basic pub snacks. This fine traditional pub's main claim to fame is the story that the Stone of Destiny was hidden in the cellar after liberation from Westminster Abbey in 1950.

The **Park Bar**

1202 Argyle Street, G3
0141 339 1715

Friendly lounge bar with strong Highland associations opposite Argyle Street's famous ash tree, not quite the Yggdrasil tree of Norse mythology, but reputed to be more than 140 years old! Good value pub lunches served Mon-Sat 12-3 and 5-8; Sun 12.30-3. Traditional Scottish folk music Wed to Sun evenings.

This section of Argyle Street was originally Westergait, a country road leading to the mills of Partick and the historic burgh of Dumbarton. In addition to malt kilns and barns, there were a number of thatched cottages at intervals along the road, mainly occupied by maltmen and small brewers. John McUre, Glasgow's first historian, mentions that the ale was 'prepared the one day, and delivered the next morning at the houses of the citizens'. Since tea and coffee were little used in 18th century Scotland, ale was the usual breakfast drink.

Allegedly, Argyle Street was named in honour of an 18th-century Duke of Argyll, whose funeral procession passed that way, en route for the family burial vault at Kilmun, on Holy Loch. The Duke's body is supposed to have lain in state in The Black Bull Inn, which stood on the site of the Argyle Street branch of Marks and Spencers' department store.

The **Partick Tavern**

165 Dumbarton Road, G11
0141 339 7571

Long-established local, now a modern café-bar. When the first edition of this book

appeared, The Partick Tavern still retained excellent art deco stained glass windows, but the current trend is towards continental-style bars with big areas of see-through glass. Laid-back customers now like to be seen eating and drinking. Traditional Scottish pubs had etched or stained glass windows because punters did not like to be seen holding up the bar. Full menu served 12-8 daily.

The **Ritz Bar**

241 North Street, G3
0141 226 4419

In the 1890s, Highland Park malt whisky was sold here at three old pennies a nip! Rich plaster cornices and cast-iron pillars survive from the original pub, which probably had a large island bar. There's also evidence of an art deco transformation at some stage in the pub's history. Warm wall panelling interspersed with mirrors and comfortably upholstered seating gives The Ritz the relaxed atmosphere of a club smoking room. Regular and guest real ales are dispensed via hand pumps. Traditional bar meals at reasonable prices. Karaoke every Sat.

Near The Ritz, at the junction of Sauchiehall Street and Woodside Crescent, is the Cameron Memorial Fountain, Glasgow's modest answer to the Leaning Tower of Pisa. This extravagant baroque structure was erected, in 1896, in memory of Charles Cameron MP, proprietor of *The North British Daily Mail.* Its neighbour was the Grand Hotel (1877), demolished to make way for the M8 and Fountain House, a ghastly 1980s office block.

The Rock

205 Hyndland Road, G12
0141 334 6977

Middle class standards of 'respectability' in the late Victorian and Edwardian periods ensured that the new suburb of Hyndland was a pub-free zone. This is therefore a comparatively modern free-standing hostelry with two bars and pseudo-Victorian decor. Meals served 11am-9pm daily.

Hyndland, mostly built between 1890 and 1910, comes as a surprise to anyone who equates the word 'tenement' with poor housing conditions. Four-storey tenements here are exceedingly handsome, with impressive features such as oriel windows and picturesque corner turrets.

The Rosevale Tavern

483 Dumbarton Road, G11

A busy and long-established Partick local at the corner of Rosevale Street. Eclectic collection of prints and portraits. Inexpensive bar lunches.

The Rubaiyat

94 Byres Road, G12
0141 341 1041

Built in the early 1950s, on the site of Drummond's Tea Rooms, this was formerly the finest hostelry in the west end, bar none. In pristine state, The Rubaiyat consisted of a cosy lounge bar and a small but exquisite circular cocktail bar ('the Bowl of Night'). In the 1980s the original interior was destroyed, despite vehement protests by angry locals, but the marvellous etched mirrors, inspired by Omar

Khayyám's famous poem, survived outwith the original decorative context. Now, with many of the area's traditional pubs being turned into continental-style café-bars, the mirrors have vanished, and The Rubaiyat is currently a trendy bar/diner. The fate of this famous hostelry highlights the deplorable lack of statutory safeguards for the nation's finest pubs. Lunch menu served 12-2.30.

Scaramouche

140 Elderslie Street, G37
0141 572 0828

A 1980s bar/bistro, in a converted Victorian stable block at the corner of Woodside Place Lane, a short walk from Sauchiehall Street. Features include a mahogany island bar, warm wall panelling, and leather-upholstered seats. Popular with office workers, whose places of toil have been ingeniously slotted into the former drawing rooms and night nurseries of the 19th-century bourgeoisie. Good value bar snacks and meals.

Tiberio Fiorelli, one of the most celebrated actors of the 17th-century Italian Commedia dell'Arte, took the stage name 'Scaramouche'. He is said to have retained his skills as a mime and acrobat until his death at the age of 90.

The **Smiddy Bar**

309 Dumbarton Road, G11
0141 576 0042

A revamped Victorian pub with original cornices and pillars in the public bar. Now a pastiche of the famous 'Glasgow Style'.

The old Partick smithy stood in this vicinity. In the mid-19th century, the village blacksmith was Will McGowan. According to a Partick historian of bygone

days, he was 'a typical village smith, whose brawny arm was of great service in the struggle which the villagers had to preserve their right-of-way to the "Stepping Stones" over the Kelvin.'

The **Snaffle Bit**

979 Sauchiehall Street, G3
0141 339 7163

Long-established basic lounge bar in Victorian terrace near Kelvingrove Museum and Art Galleries. The interior reflects the 1960s enthusiasm for mock-Tudor. Real ales are on tap, along with inexpensive meals and snacks.

The **Stirling Castle**

90 Old Dumbarton Road, G3
0141 339 8132

Popular local, near the Art Galleries and Museum of Transport. Often frequented by nervous expectant fathers from the nearby maternity hospital at Yorkhill. The wood-panelled interior is enhanced by mirrors and eclectic bric-a-brac. Adjoining lounge/diner. Full menu served 12-9.30 daily.

Stravaigin

26 Gibson Street, G12
0141 334 2665

To stravaig is 'to roam, wander idly, gad about in an aimless casual manner', perhaps ending up at this informal café-bar/restaurant, near the University of Glasgow. Slender cast iron columns support the bar

ceiling, and a spiral staircase leads to a mezzanine floor. With well-kept real ale, a good selection of malts and wines by the glass, and well-prepared meals served in both bar and downstairs restaurant, one could stravaig further and fare much worse. Food available Sun-Thur till 10.30pm; Fri-Sat till 11.30pm.

Stumps

7 Peel Street, G11
0141 339 2537

Until 1995, this was The Manhattan, a wonderfully loopy 1950s lounge bar. The interior was painted in shades of pink and artificial windows looked out on a vintage Manhattan townscape. Behind the bar, there was a midnight blue backdrop of New York skyscrapers. The present bar, though comfortable, lacks the eccentric character of its predecessor. There are some prints of local interest, and the cricketing theme acknowledges the traditions of this locality. In the mid 19th-century, two clubs, the Clutha and the Royal, shared a pitch at Hamilton Crescent (now Fortrose Street). In 1862 some of the Clutha players formed the West of Scotland Cricket Club.

The Tap

1055 Sauchiehall Street, G3
0141 339 0643

Two Victorian tenement houses were transformed into this popular bar and lounge, formerly known as The Brewery Tap. Large windows face Kelvingrove Park and Glasgow University. The Tap, directly opposite University Avenue, is student-friendly and the lounge houses a pool

table and big screen TV. Lunch served 12-3 daily; night bites such as pizzas 5-9. Live music every Fri-Sat. Handy for Kelvingrove Art Galleries and Museum.

Tennent's

191 Byres Road, G12
0141 341 1024

In 1871, Hugh Tennent Jnr, a grandson of Wellpark Brewery's Hugh Tennent, established the Wellshot Brewery at Cambuslang. He later severed his connection with the Cambuslang venture, and commenced as a wine and spirit merchant, opening pubs in Glasgow, Rutherglen, Whiteinch and Clydebank. His Byres Road pub is still going strong, though sadly no longer dispensing the 'Royal Brackla' single malt whisky from polished wooden barrels as in Hugh's day. Heavy cornices and columns with foliated capitals hint at past Victorian glories. There's a rotating selection of cask-conditioned ales, and the clientele ranges from boisterous students to philosophical old-timers. Good value bar lunches. DJs in the basement bar Thu-Sun. Hugh Tennent Jnr would be delighted to know that his pub is still, in the early 21st century, a much-appreciated local amenity.

The Thornwood

722-4 Dumbarton Road, G11
0141 339 0836

Formerly a classic *art moderne* lounge bar, with an exterior of primrose and black vitrolite and a neon-lit fascia. The 'streamlined' interior was remarkably evocative of its period, with dark walnut veneered panelling and sunken ceiling lights.

The present interior follows the exact alignment of the original bar, but predictable mock-Victorian touches do little to compensate for sophisticated 1930s styling. Pubs of any description are a rarity in this neck of the woods, since

in 1920 the good people of Whiteinch voted to become 'dry' under the 'Local Veto' provisions of the Temperance (Scotland) Act of 1913. Bar snacks served 12-6. Karaoke on Sats.

A famous inn, known as Granny Gibb's Cottage, once stood on the site of the Thornwood roundabout. Kept by widow Elizabeth Gibb and her daughters, it had been built in 1796 by her husband. The inn was a favourite resort of West Highland cattle drovers who rested there en route to the Glasgow cattle market. Granny Gibbs was a strict Sabbatarian who didn't permit the punters to arrive or depart on the Lord's Day.

The **Three Judges**

141 Dumbarton Road, G11
0141 337 3055

This is one of Glasgow's premier real ale outlets purveying a range of regular and rotating guest ales. Most of the available wall space is covered by beer mats advertising ales which have been sold here over the years. The Three Judges used to be popular with the boxing fraternity and owes its present name to pugilistic associations, but in the early 1900s it was The Tower Bar, owned by James L Bennett, member of a well-known firm of whisky merchants. The rear wall is adorned with an attractive Edwardian mirror, advertising the Bennett Brothers' Old Liqueur Whisky and decorated with a gold-engraved version of their tower trademark. Summertime jazz is played here every Sunday afternoon.

Partick Bridge Street, at this corner, commemorates the old Partick bridge, built in the 17th century. In the

early 19th century, two famous Partick hostelries stood near the bridge: The Ark and The Old Bridge Inn. As with the rival Bun and Yill House, The Old Bridge Inn served duck dinners to tourists from Glasgow.

Two Ways

1004 Argyle Street, G3

This friendly unpretentious local has long been celebrated as the haven of Govan philosopher Rab C Nesbit, his cronies and relations. In reality, it's a fair distance from Govan – and on the opposite bank of the Clyde from that much-maligned faubourg. In bygone days, however, Rab's grandpaw could have travelled here without too much trouble, using either the original Clyde Tunnel or the Glasgow District Subway – the Subway's redundant Finnieston station used to be situated directly opposite the pub.

In the late-1880s, this long-established pub belonged to spirit merchants Peter Buchanan and James Scott, proprietors of several well-run city pubs, including The Blane Valley in Glassford Street (see entry). Whisky casks stood on a platform behind the semi-circular bar. Now a well-preserved authentic 50s lounge bar, taking its name from its location – at the junction of Kent Road and Argyle Street.

Uisge Beatha

232 Woodlands Road, G3
0141 564 1596

There was once a strong Scottish tradition of 'museum' pubs. Victorian bar-owners took pleasure in cramming their hostelries with conversation pieces – everything from mounted stag heads to martial souvenirs of 'Queen Victoria's little wars'. The tradition lives on in Uisge Beatha's three eccentrically-furnished rooms, crammed with paintings and artefacts, including a sobering effigy of Baroness Thatcher. The good value menu features

traditional Scottish dishes such as haggis, neeps and tatties. 'Uisge beatha' ('water of life') is represented by an extensive selection of single malts, and real ale is on tap. In the early 1990s, this pub, a west end institution, sold ales from the Glaschu Brewery – a micro-brewery which closed in 1996 after local residents complained about the aroma from brewing mash.

Upstairs at the Chip

12 Ashton Lane, G12
0141 334 5007

Civilised bar/bistro in The Ubiquitous Chip, a famous west end restaurant popular with media folk. Sells real ales, a good range of malt whiskies and wide selection of wines by the glass. There's a long bar, peat fire (in season), wooden rafters, and walls of painted brick. Food is served all day, and the menu includes traditional Scottish fare.

Handy for the Botanic Gardens, which moved to this vicinity in 1842. The most remarkable feature of the Gardens is the Kibble Palace. John Kibble erected the original conservatory at Coulport on Loch Long, in the 1860s. He subsequently offered it to Glasgow, as a palace of art and concert hall. It was rebuilt in the Botanic Gardens in 1872. Kibble retained free use of the building for 21 years, during which it became a popular venue for concerts and social functions. The city took over in 1887. Embellished with bleached white sculptures, the Palace is one of Glasgow's most quintessentially Victorian sights.

The **Victoria Bar**

336 Dumbarton Road, G11
0141 339 1000

A photograph dating from 1931 shows this friendly Partick local to have been a well-preserved Victorian pub at that time, with virtuoso lettering and elaborate etched glass. Shortly afterwards it was remodelled in art deco style with a bar for men and a small lounge for mixed couples. Such bars were a concession to changing social attitudes: the men-only pub was, slowly but surely, on the way out, though it would take sex discrimination legislation to administer the *coup-de-grâce*. Refurbished in 1996, the pub retains the layout of its pre-war counterpart, though the style is now pseudo-Victorian.

The **Windsor Tavern**

473 Dumbarton Road, G11
0141 569 1011

Long-established and well-run Partick lounge bar. In the 1890s the original Windsor was an upmarket licensed restaurant with a rich late-Victorian interior. It was popular with salaried staff employed in D and W Henderson's Meadowside Shipyard (previously Tod and McGregor's). One of the regulars was the famous yacht designer George L Watson.

Wintersgill's

226 Great Western Road, G4
0141 332 3532

Originally a Samuel Dow pub, this old-established howff underwent alterations in the 1930s, when lounge bars came into vogue. By 1939, the basement housed an art deco cocktail bar, with stylised representations of trendy cocktails such as White Lady, Manhattan and Angel's Kiss. Wintergill's no longer has pretentions to Jazz Age sophistication. It's now a popular no-frills local. Basic pub grub. Live music every Thu. Karaoke every Fri-Sat.

Constructed in 1841, Great Western Road is Glasgow's longest thoroughfare (Duke Street being the longest street). The section from Botanic Gardens to Anniesland Toll became the west end's *via triumphalis*, lined with stately villas and mansions.

Whistler's Mother

116 Byres Road, G12
0141 576 0528

Vibrant cosmopolitan bistro, frequented by Byres Road's chattering classes. Breakfast served 10 am till 12 noon. Lunch menu 12 noon-4.30. Evening meals 5-9 Sun-Thur; 5-10 Fri-Sat.

There are two places above all others to study the work of James McNeill Whistler: the Freer Gallery of Art in Washington D C, and the Hunterian Gallery, on University Avenue, a short distance from this bar. At the Hunterian you can also see the artist's

painting equipment and the furniture and porcelain he collected.

Wolbirn's Wharf

26 Yoker Ferry Road, G14
0141 959 2016

Opened in 1990, this attractive riverside hostelry incorporates a long derelict ferrymaster's house. Bric-a-brac is much in evidence, and the amenities include a beer garden. Good value menu served seven days a week. Adventurous pilgrims can take the only surviving Clyde ferry to The Ferry Inn, on the south (Renfrew) bank of the river. The original Ferry Inn and Cyclists' Rest was on the north (Yoker) bank, and was a little cottage with a thatched roof.

In the 1890s, the heyday of the cycling craze, the Inn featured in a journal called *The Scottish Cyclist* – which pointed out that 'west-end wheelmen' used the Inn when cycling, via the ferry, to Dumbarton or Helensburgh.

Central Glasgow is lucky to exist. It might well have been reduced to rubble in a few hours during WW2 – like Coventry or Clydebank. It came perilously close to extinction after the war, when ambitious planners proposed to make up for the Luftwaffe's deficiencies, raze the entire city, and turn Glasgow into 'the most modern city in Europe' – a radial metropolis of concrete towers and flyovers, with rooftop helipads. Despite the loss of many fine individual buildings, the inner city fortunately escaped the kind of reconstruction that devastated Birmingham, Manchester, Leeds and Liverpool – to make a profound impression on Sir John Betjeman and other astute observers in the 1960s, by which time Glasgow was being described as 'the Victorian city par excellence'. But the admiration of a few enlightened commentators in that era didn't prevent highway engineers from completing the north and west flanks of an urban motorway, the Inner Ring Road. Certainly things might have been much worse. The unexecuted east flank of the motorway would have been routed south from the Townhead interchange more or less on the line of High Street, sweeping past the Cathedral – Scotland's finest Gothic building – on concrete piloti and vitually annihilating Glasgow Green, Britain's oldest civic park.

At its proud commercial core, Victorian and Edwardian Glasgow was truly 'no mean city': the building materials were freestone and granite and architects – most of them local men who knew and loved their city – drew inspiration from sources as diverse as Ancient Egypt and Renaissance Italy. In recent years, many of the finest palaces of commerce in the city centre have been turned into pubs, and magnificent banking halls where a cathedral silence was once *de rigueur* are now filled with noise and bustle.

The **Admiral**

72a Waterloo Street, G2
0141 221 7705

It's a mystery why Lord Nelson presides over this pub, instead of the Iron Duke. Perhaps the owners have confused Trafalgar with Waterloo. This is a comfortable mock-Victorian lounge bar, an agreeable oasis

in a business district comparatively devoid of pubs. Moderately priced bar food.

A few yards away, at 64 Waterloo Street, there's a remarkable monument to the great age of Victorian 'whisky barons'. Wright and Greig Ltd, a Glasgow firm of distillers and blenders, were proprietors of the popular 'Roderick Dhu' brand, inspired by the outlawed Highland chieftain in Sir Walter Scott's poem *The Lady of the Lake*. In 1898, they erected a prestigious office building in Waterloo Street, decorating the ornate red sandstone ediface with statues of the principal characters in the poem.

All Bar One

62-72 St Vincent Street, G2
0141 229 6060

Informal glass-fronted café-bar on two levels, opened in 1999. One of a chain designed specifically as 'women friendly' leisure spaces. At lunchtime the Glasgow branch attracts office personnel and shoppers. The mezzanine floor offers fine views of Victorian townscape. Excellent selection of wines. Bar open : Mon-Sat 11am-midnight; Sun 12.30pm-midnight.

The **Ark**

46 North Frederick Street, G1
0141 559 4331

Ultra-modern bar complex and beer garden, catering mainly for students from nearby seats of learning, including Strathclyde University. If Latin was still the students' lingua franca, this area would be the town's Latin Quarter. Opposite The Ark, the Corbusean Glasgow College of Building and Printing harks back to the early 1960s, when 'the cult of the new' was in the ascendant, magnificent Victorian buildings were being bulldozed out of existence, tower blocks were the last word in public housing, and urban motorways were the height of fashion. Breakfast served 11-12; full menu 12-7; Sunday lunch 12-6.

The **Atholl**

134 Renfield Street, G2
0141 332 2541

In the 1920s, this hostelry, now a popular café-bar, was known as The Criterion Restaurant and fragments of the original stained glass remain. Handy for Buchanan Street Bus Station, the Glasgow Royal Concert Hall, and the new £27 million UGC 18-screen cinema, the biggest movie complex in Scotland. Good value meals and snacks.

The Pavilion Theatre opposite, built in 1904, was originally named the Palace of Varieties. It had a novel feature – a sliding roof which could be opened on fine summer evenings. Many great stars of the Edwardian music hall performed here, sole reminder that this area was once Glasgow's 'theatreland'.

The **Auctioneers**

6 North Court, G1
0141 229 5851

North Court runs from St Vincent Place to Royal Exchange Square, and this bar/diner is handy for George Square and the Gallery of Modern Art. It opened in the late 1990s in Victorian premises which formerly did duty as the auction rooms of Robert McTear & Co, an old-established firm of city auctioneers. The present pub displays copious bric-a-brac in memory of bygone days. Some relics of the original interiors, including rich cornices and cast-iron pillars with ornate capitals, can also be seen. Some of the seating here is arranged in intimate booths and alcoves. A good variety of meals and snacks are available. Sunday brunch, 12.30-4. DJs Saturdays from 8pm.

The **Baby Grand**

7 Elmbank Gardens, G2
0141 226 3800

Handy for the King's Theatre and Mitchell Library, this well-hidden American-style bar/diner attracts many office workers at lunchtimes. Opposite Charing Cross low-level railway station, it can be approached via Bath Street or Elmbank Crescent. Food is served from 8am until midnight (1am at weekends), and there's live music most nights of the week.

Bacchus

80 Glassford Street, G1
0141 572 0080

Trendy 1990s café-bar with mural-decorated walls, named in honour of the Roman god of wine. Male and female groupies of the god took part in the 'bacchanal' – a drunken

and orgiastic celebration. Food, ranging from pakora and stir-fries to burgers and bangers and mash, available from opening time until 7pm. The basement can be reserved for parties and there's a DJ Mon-Thur.

In 1798, Mr Henderson, dentist, Glassford Street, promised to set 'snaggled teeth' straight, providing that the patient was not 'past a certain age'.

Balsa

71 Renfield Street, G2
0141 333 9725

Formerly Brahms and Liszt, a popular student haunt where candlelight helped create a cosy atmosphere, this subterranean café-bar was refurbished in 1999. The new bar, situated beneath De Quincey's (see entry), has three seating areas, and the decor is minimalist, with rubber-tiled floors, blond wood, colourful plastic seats, and printed muslin wall hangings decorated with the ubiquitous Balsa 'B'.

Balsa's menu ranges from Sicilian lasagne and Tuscan bolognese to haggis, neeps and tatties. Premium lager beers are on offer, along with absinthe, that favourite tipple of late-Victorian decadents. DJs Wed-Sun. Happy hours from 5-8pm every evening.

The Bank

23 Queen Street, G1
0141 248 4455

Long-established and well-patronised bar/diner with a low-ceilinged interior and traditional decor, good prints, and restrained use of bric-a-brac. Extensive lunch menu. Evening set menu available from 7pm.

The original Bank

Restaurant was situated at 35 Queen Street. The premises belonged to Andrew Stark until 1889, when they were acquired by an Austrian called Brunfaut, late of Vienna, Berlin, Mentone, and Nice. He transformed the establishment: the dining room was adorned with paintings inspired by Sir Walter Scott's poem *The Lady of the Lake* and Austrian and Bavarian draught lager beers were a speciality of the house.

In the 1890s, The Bank Restaurant was one of the city's most popular hostelries, with football teams frequently dining there after matches. As late as the 1960s, when it was owned by Willie Maley, a former Celtic FC manager, it had strong sporting connections. The old Bank Restaurant may have been named after the National Bank of Scotland (1847), a sumptuous Italian palazzo which stood at 57 Queen Street until 1901, when it was taken down and re-erected within Queen's Park as Langside Halls. But in early Victorian times, there was a Bank Tavern in Trongate, frequented by the town's literati.

The **Bar**

396 Sauchiehall Street, G2

Popular glass-fronted café-bar with youthful clientele. Food served Mon-Sat 12 noon till 8pm. Regular drinks promos.

In 1862, 'New Turkish Baths' opened in fashionable Sauchiehall Street. One bath cost 2/6d – but patrons could have ten ablutions for a quid. This famous street still had plenty of style in 1933, when the official *City Guide* observed that 'Within the georgeous and impressive salons of Sauchiehall Street ... the latest creations of the Rue de la Paix are to be seen, *objets d'art* from every corner of the globe are there for the collector to acquire, and when from a surfeit of luxury the shopper desires a few well earned moments of rest, the numerous cafés, lounges and tearooms offer their welcome invitation.'

Bar 10

10 Mitchell Lane, G1
0141 243 2099

Minimalist continental-style café-bar, opened in the early 1990s. Located in a converted warehouse, it's convenient for Buchanan Street shopping precinct and the new Lighthouse, Scotland's Centre for Architecture. Young artists can use Bar 10 as an exhibition space with no commission taken on works sold. Popular with all age groups by day. Younger evening clientele. An attractive lunchtime rendezvous offering an inexpensive and varied café menu. Regular DJs.

Bar Ce Lona

427 Sauchiehall Street, G2
0141 332 2528

Like Bar Gaudi in nearby Blythswood Street, this new pub/restaurant pays homage to the idiosyncratic style of the great Catalan architect Gaudi. The bar features regular DJs. Bar snacks are creative and inexpensive, and a set-price pre-theatre menu is available from 5-7pm.

Bar **Gaudi**

118a Blythswood Street, G2
0141 572 0834

Until recently, this tiny pub was a mock-Tudor hostelry dating from the early 1970s.

The pub's regulars – folk of mature years – were immortalised in a mural behind the bar. The present pub was inspired by the avant-garde architect Antoni Gaudi – who never, as far as is known, set foot in Blythswood Street. The revamped interior is intimate and pleasant, and the bar staff are welcoming and friendly. Breakfast is served from 8pm; lunch 12-3; dinner 5 till 9. DJs Tuesday and Thursday-Saturday. Regular DJs. Happy hours: 5-8pm daily.

The **Bay Horse**

19 Bath Street, G2
0141 332 0761

Until the early 1990s The Bay Horse retained the characteristics of an interwar lounge bar, with a fine range of art deco stained glass windows from that era. By the time the first edition of this book appeared, it had been remodelled in pseudo-Victorian fashion. Art deco glass survives in the vestibule, and the pub retains the unpretentious character of an old-fashioned Glesca 'men's shoap', where serious communion with the refreshments involves standing at the bar. Basic pub snacks are served. Handy for the Royal Concert Hall and the Buchanan Galleries.

The **Beresford**

468 Sauchiehall Street, G2
0141 332 8434

A small unpretentious lounge bar situated in the former Beresford Hotel, now Strathclyde University's Baird Hall of Residence. The Beresford Hotel, named after its enterprising owner/architect W Beresford

Inglis, opened in 1938, in time for Glasgow's Empire Exhibition, which attracted 12.5 million visitors to Bellahouston Park. Faience-clad in bright colours, and impeccably 'streamlined' in *art moderne* fashion, the Beresford Hotel would not have looked out of place in 1930s Florida. Inglis also designed the hotel's smart cocktail bar – which closed when the hotel went out of business after WW2. It was placed in charge of a Canadian-born barman who had mixed cocktails in top London nightspots.

Bonaparte's

Central Station, G1
0141 221 9205

Napoleon Bonaparte's Old Guard charged with matchless *élan*, and charging £2.50 for a small bottle of lager, the proprietors of Bonaparte's are not doing too badly themselves. French windows lead to a sweeping balcony overlooking the concourse of one of Europe's most impressive railway terminals, originally built for the Caledonian Railway Company. You can sit here and watch the world go by, or alternatively, look up and admire the magnificent roof canopy – a *tour de force* of Scottish engineering at the end of the 19th century.

Boogie Bar

261 Hope Street, G1
0141 331 1886

Gay-friendly bar, opened in 2000. Open noon-midnight Mon-Sat. Food served noon-7.30 pm. Clientele: mixed young crowd.

The **Brew House**

84 West Nile Street, G1

This pub was already well-established in 1886 when a new proprietor, James Cook, named it The Red Lion. It retained that name until the late 1990s. The original Red Lion was renowned for its welsh rarebit pub snacks. It had a dignified frontage, illuminated at night by a large stained-glass lamp, suspended on an ornate iron bracket. The interior was handsome, with a marble fireplace and richly carved bar fittings.

As happens all the time in 'post-industrial' Glasgow, a fine old pub with interesting traditions has been given a 'branded' corporate image and divested of character. Inexpensive pub lunches. Live music Tues. Karaoke Wed-Thur. DJs Fri-Sat.

Brunswick Cellars

239 Sauchiehall Street, G2

0141 572 0016

No front or fascia here, just a door in the wall which draws you into an atmospheric low-ceilinged subterranean howff. There are perils for the near-sighted, but the ambience is relaxed and friendly. Handy for the Glasgow Film Theatre in nearby Rose Street.

Buchanan's

72 Howard Street, G1

0141 226 8431

Until 1999, this unpretentious modern bar was The New Eagle Inn, named after The Eagle Inn, a long-established Howard Street hostelry, demolished in 1977. The original Eagle Inn and Renfrewshire Hotel, demolished at the end of the 19th century, was in Maxwell Street. Its courtyard was a venue for cock-fights, on which huge sums were wagered. Beer and spirits are sold here at rock-bottom prices.

Budda

142a St Vincent Street, G2

0141 221 5660

This trendy bar/restaurant is located in 'The Hatrack' (1900-02), a remarkable art nouveau skyscraper.

This section of St Vincent

Street originally consisted of town houses, and 'the Hatrack', ten storeys high, was built on a single house plot, hence its extreme attentuation. DJs Thursday-Sunday; Happy hours: Sun-Mon 4-7.30pm. Sun-Thur drinks promos.

Café **Cine**

81 Renfield Street, G2
0141 353 2807

Well-established continental-style café-bar. Café Cine serves a cosmopolitan menu from noon until 7pm. DJs Wed-Sun. Handy for the

Odeon cinema. Originally the Paramount, this *art moderne* super-cinema (1935) was restored externally – complete with neon tube lights – in 1999.

Café **Source**

1 St Andrew's Square
0141 548 6020

Located in the sunk storey of St Andrew's Church, this café bar/bistro is a welcome addition to a historic area which is not over-endowed with attractive bars and restaurants. Snacks, lunches and evening meals are served, and there are live music sessions (folk and jazz) on Wednesday evenings.

The **Cask and Still**

154 Hope Street, G2
0141 333 0980

This long-established traditional pub was owned in the 1870s by a spirit merchant called William McCall. Handy for Central Station, it's a mecca for connoisseurs of 'the cratur'. The ornate gantry accommodates more than 500 malts and blended whiskies, including limited bottlings, and a bargain price Malt of

the Month. Cask-conditioned ales are on tap, including weekly changing guest ales. Good value bar meals served at lunchtimes.

Cathedral House
Hotel

28 Cathedral Square, G4
0141 552 3519

Situated directly opposite Glasgow Necropolis, burial ground of the city's Victorian merchants and industrialists, this Victorian neo-baronial building (1894-96) was formerly the premises of the Discharged Prisoners Aid Society. The café-bar interior is wood-panelled and on three levels and the relaxed ambience is enhanced by evening candlelight. There's a traditional long bar with an elegant pedimented gantry, decorative ironwork and good-quality bar furniture. Varied and well-presented bar meals and snacks. À la carte restaurant upstairs.

Until 1958, Duke Street prison for women, built in the 1820s on the site of the old 'Bridewell' or House of Correction for vagrants and prostitutes, stood on the site of the present Ladywell housing estate. A section of the prison wall has been preserved in the High Street. Originally both sexes were incarcerated in Duke Street prison and executions took place on an open scaffold within the walls.

While you are in this vicinity, pause to look at Provand's Lordship (1471), now a museum. Of the well-built manses and houses which once clustered around the Cathedral in pre-Reformation times, Provand's Lordship, Glasgow's oldest house, is the only survivor. Mary Queen of Scots reputedly stayed in this stone-built dwelling in 1567, when she came to Glasgow to visit the ailing Lord Darnley. By the early 1900s, the building had fallen into disrepair and part of it was an alehouse. It was restored in 1906.

Many old taverns were situated in this part of the city, which was eventually transformed by the Improvement Trust. In the early 19th century, a tavern called The Green Cellars stood near the public washing and bleaching green on the banks of the Molendinar Burn, south of the Cathedral.

The **Clutha Vaults**

167-169 Stockwell Street, G1
0141 552 7520

In the 1890s, this pub sold 1858 cognac, Moët et Chandon champagne, Allsopp's, Bass and Melvin's ales, and the Clutha Blend of whisky. Now there's a cosy Victorian-style interior with low, beamed ceiling and wood-panelled walls adorned with photographs of old Gorbals. Basic inexpensive pub menu.

'Clutha' is an old name for the Clyde. 'Cluthas' were also little twin-screw steamers which operated a penny service between Victoria Bridge and Whiteinch. The Clyde Navigation Trust started the service to undercut horse-drawn trams, which were slower and charged 4d for the same journey. Services began in

1884. Eventually, 12 vessels were engaged on the run of over three miles, operating at fifteen-minute intervals with calls at eleven landing stages en route. In 1898, the introduction of electric tram-cars – so fast they were dubbed 'scooshcaurs' – challenged the Cluthas and their services terminated in 1903. One drawback of travel by river boat was the smell. By the early 1900s, an intolerable stench rose from the heavily-polluted Clyde in hot weather.

Stockwell Street, formerly Stockwellgait, reputedly took its name from a public well, operated by a wooden stock. Known in mediaeval times as Fishergait – the way to the salmon fishers' village by the Clyde – it was the chief entrance to the city from the south and many wealthy merchants lived there. The Stockwell mansion of George Johnson, the last surviving 17th-century mansion in the city, was demolished as recently as 1976.

In the 18th century, Stockwell Street's southern end witnessed regular Saturday-night 'bickers' between the inhabitants of Glasgow and natives of Gorbals. Both sides fought to gain control of an islet situated in the middle of the shallow river, opposite the present Carlton Place.

Corinthian

191 Ingram Street, G1
0141 552 1101

Opened appropriately in City of Architecture Year 1999, Corinthian doubtlessly takes its name from the third classical order of architecture. Glasgow's leisure industry, one of the outstanding success stories of the last several decades, has come to the rescue of many fine buildings, not least the former Union Bank of Scotland which now houses Corinthian. The original Glasgow Union Bank was founded in Virginia Street in 1830. In 1841 a new bank was built on the site of the famous Virginia Mansion. It was remodelled internally in the 1850s, and in the 1870s given a superb Italianate palazzo façade. When the bank eventually closed, the building became Lanarkshire House and latterly accommodated the High Court of Justiciary.

Now the former Union

Bank houses a £5m complex boasting four bars, a restaurant, five function/conference rooms, a nightclub and private suites. The sensational main bar, occupying the former bank telling room, is Glasgow's most sumptuous 'superpub'. The vast room, with coved ceiling, is surmounted by a splendid dome filled with leaded glass. To delight the eye there are also elaborate plaster friezes, pediments and ceilings, huge mirrors in gilded frames, and astounding electroliers (the sort that rich, vulgar Pompeiians would surely have acquired if they had been able to harness electricity). Seating is arranged in semi-private nooks. A tasty snack menu is available from noon until 9.30 pm.

In the impressive barrel-vaulted restaurant, lunch is served Sun-Fri, noon-3 pm; dinner Mon-Sun, 5.30-11pm. The basement nightclub 'Life', open until 3 am Thur-Sat, occupies the High Court's former jail cells and features soft leather sofas set amid stone columns and arches. The Cocktail and Piano bars once accommodated the Procurator Fiscal and the Clerks of the Court. The former offers a wide selection of traditional and contemporary cocktails (half price Fri-Sat between 5pm and 7 pm) while the latter features pianists playing ragtime, jazz, etc in an avuncular manner.

The **Corn Exchange**

88 Gordon Street, G1
0141 248 5380

This is the first pub many people see when they arrive at Glasgow's Central Station. Food is served Mon-Wed noon-11pm; Thu-Sat noon-midnight; Sun 12.30-11pm and office workers, rail travellers and shoppers can take advantage of cheap bar lunches.

In the 1890s, The Corn Exchange Restaurant, a great favourite with city merchants, occupied this site. It was still a famous Glasgow lunch venue in the 1940s. Like the present pub, it took its name from the Corn Exchange, a handsome French Renaissance-style building, formerly located in Hope Street. Though listed, the Corn Exchange was demolished in the 1960s. The first Glasgow Corn Exchange was established in 1842, a time of great distress among the poor. Crowds massed on Glasgow Green, listened to impassioned Chartist oratory, and demanded 'work and bread'.

The **Counting House**

2 St Vincent Street, G1
0141 248 9568

The English-based JD Wetherspoon chain's Glasgow flagship 'superpub' occupies one of the city's finest and most monumental Italianate palazzi – J T Rochead's Bank of Scotland (1867-70). Much of the original decor survives, and the central drinking space – the bank's double-height telling room – is most impressive, with a glazed dome and rows of caryatids. As befits a pub in such a grand building and in a central location, The Counting House is extremely popular. In the tourist season, the clientele is cosmopolitan. There's a large no-smoking area here – and a complete absence of obtrusive music. The menu is varied and

inexpensive, and, as in other Wetherspoon establishments, there's a fine range of well-kept real ales.

George Square, overlooked by The Counting House, was laid out in 1781 and named after George III. According to an old authority, it was originally 'a hollow filled with green water and a favourite resort for drowning puppies and cats.' Between 1789 and the 1820s, three-storey terraces houses were built around the edges of the Square. Until well into the 19th century, sheep grazed in the grassy centre, which was railed off as a private garden. An early view of the Square shows servant women hanging out washing and beating carpets. Residents included Patrick Colquhoun, tobacco and cotton merchant, and prime mover in setting up Glasgow's Chamber of Commerce (1783), the first in the UK. In 1836, at 'Mr Gullan's Academy', George Square, 'young ladies' were taught 'grammar and composition, geography, and the use of the Globes'.

The Square opened to the public in 1876. By the end of the 19th century, its scale had been changed by Victorian buildings, including the City Chambers (1882-90) and it was the town's Valhalla, full of statues of the good and the great.

The **Crystal Palace**

36 Jamaica Street, G1
0141 221 2624

Opened in 2000 at a cost of £3m, this is another J D Wetherspoon superpub' in a listed building, dating from 1855-56, when cast-iron and plate glass were at the cutting edge of building technology. In 1851, Great Britain led the world in 'ferrovitreous' construction with the Crystal Palace in London's Hyde Park, designed to house the Great Exhibition of All Nations. Unlike the late and unlamented Millennium Dome, the Crystal Palace was filled to overflowing with fascinating objects from the four corners of the globe – including the Koh-i-Noor diamond from India and repeating firearms from the USA. In the aftermath of the Exhibition, a number of elegant iron-framed warehouses graced the streets of Glasgow. In designing Gardner's furniture warehouse in Jamaica Street, John Baird exploited the exciting possibilities of the new materials and the result was a delightful structure – an airy Venetian palazzo in cast-iron and glass.

The pub, which boasts wheelchair accessibility, is on two levels, with a bar on each level. Both levels have large non-smoking areas, and, as with all Wetherspoon outlets, the premises are music-free with a ban on pool tables. Bar furniture is trendy – metal with *faux* zebra skin seats. A few photographic reproductions pay lip-service to the Hyde Park Crystal Palace and its designer, Joseph Paxton. The Crystal Palace theme could have been more prominent here. Food (12 till late) and drink are up to the usual high Wetherspoon standards, with a good choice of real ales and a varied and reliable menu.

Denholm's Bar

17 Hope Street, G2
0141 221 3016

A long-established traditional city pub, convenient for Central Station, featuring an attractive wood-panelled interior with long bar and gantry. In its 1930s heyday, it was owned by Donald Boyd Denholm. Food served 11am-3pm daily.

De Quincey's

71 Renfield Street, G2
0141 333 9725

After a brief spell as The Old Rangoon, this pub has reverted to its former name. In the early 19th century, Thomas de Quincey, the celebrated English essayist and 'opium eater' rented rooms in a house on this site. The listed Victorian interior, resplendent in Burmantoft faience, was formerly the telling room of the Prudential Assurance Company, built in 1886-90. Handy for the Odeon cinema. Happy hours Mon-Thur 4-11; Fri 12-8. Closed on Sundays.

Dow Jones

203 Buchanan Street, G1
0141 332 1187

Formerly Butler's, this small, informal hostelry is handy for the Buchanan Galleries shopping centre and the Royal Concert Hall. Inexpensive basic bar menu. The interior is typical of 1990s pseudo-Victorian

trends, with traditional fireplace and bar screens. Outside the pub, a hanging sign depicts the coat of arms of God's Own Country. There can't be many people in our stocks-and-shares obsessed universe who do not know that 'the Dow-Jones' – named after two American financial staticians – is the USA's daily index of stock-exchange prices. Glasgow's own High Victorian stock exchange, richly adorned with representations of Trade and Commerce, Science, Art, Building, Mining and Engineering, is located a short distance south of this pub.

Drouthy Neebors

136 Queen Street, G1
0141 221 9330

Until recently, Doctor Brown's, and previously a Yate's Wine Lodge, this was originally The Ingram Bar. Inexpensive meals served noon-4pm. Handy for the Gallery of Modern Art.

Queen Street was formerly Cow Loan, a muddy track which left Westergait (Argyle Street) and followed the line of present-day Dundas Street to the town's cattle pastures at Cowcaddens. It was by Cow Loan that Cromwell entered the town, in 1650. From the late 18th century, the street's grandest feature was the Cunninghame mansion (1778), built by William Cunninghame of Lainshaw, the only tobacco lord to profit from the American War of Independence. When the colonies revolted, the price of tobacco rose from 3d to 6d per pound. Other Virginia merchants, believing the British would soon quell the rebellion, sold their stocks to Cunninghame. As the forces of the Crown suffered defeat, the price of tobacco rose to 3s 6d a pound. Cunninghame sold his entire stock at an enormous profit.

The Drum and Monkey

93 St Vincent Street, G2
0141 221 6636

Popular bar/bistro, a few minutes' walk from Central Station, situated in the former Bank of Scotland Chambers (1924-26). A huge armorial doorpiece provides this atmospheric hostelry, one of the first in the city to be accommodated in a listed building, with an appropriately theatrical entrance.

The interior is dark and rich with ceiling mouldings, wall panelling, a curved bar, and comfortable couches and chaise lounges. Basic bar food is available at lunchtimes with a more varied menu in the tiny restaurant. In the evenings, the restaurant goes à la carte, with a Scottish flavour.

Edward's

410 Sauchiehall Street, G2
0141 333 1138

Now one of the Edward's chain of bars, this was formerly Maxaluna, an award-winning bar/restaurant. Varied menu, including all-day breakfast, available until around 7pm. Happy hours daily between

5-8pm. DJs Thurs-Sat from 8.30pm.

Fat Boab's

40 Howard Street, G1
0141 229 5841

Friendly bogus vernacular hostelry, with low ceilings and bare wood floors. As is customary in such establishments, 'distressed' plaster wall surfaces are finished in nicotine yellow and adorned with old photographs. A separate snug bar recalls the vanished era of discreet 'carry outs'. Handy for the St

Enoch Centre and very popular, not least because of good value bar meals and snacks, served 12-7pm. Karaoke and discos Sat-Sun.

Finnegan's Wake

79 St Vincent Street, G2
0141 248 4989

A century ago, this was a popular restaurant owned by Daniel Brown. It was refurbished in 1982 as Daniel Brown's, a trendy wine bar. In the 1990s fashions changed and it became an Irish theme pub with a split-level interior plastered with authentic ephemera. The 'wallpaper' consists of Irish broadsheets, while the windows feature a selection of groceries. Irish menu and music, usually with an appropriately Hibernian flavour, at least five nights a week.

The Finnegan's Wake theme pubs take their name from a comic Irish ballad. Tim Finnegan, a hod carrier who was overfond of whiskey, fell off his ladder and was killed, so:

They wrapped him up in a
nice clean sheet,
and layed him out upon
the bed,
With a gallon of whiskey at
his feet,
and a barrel of porter at
his head.

When his friends assembled at the wake, they got drunk and fell out. In the ensuing fracas, a noggin of whiskey was spilled on Tim's corpse. Tim revived, and mourned the waste of good whiskey:

'Fling your whiskey round
like blazes, thunderin'
Jaysus,
did you think me dead?'

Flares
see 70s Revival Bar

Fouquet's

7 Renfield Street, G2
0141 226 4958

Basement bar/restaurant with three bars and a separate dining area, long popular as a venue for office parties and similar junkets.

Appetising menu served until 9.30 every night except Sun. DJs Wed-Sun. Happy hours Fri-Sat 4-8pm.

Goose on Union Street

48 Union Street, G1
Union Street
0141 229 6010

Bustling 1990s chain pub on two levels, offering a good selection of real ales and inexpensive pub food. Handy for Central Station.

Union's Street's most astonishing architectural sight, Alexander Thomson's Egyptian Halls (1871-3), is located a short distance north of this pub, on the same side of the street, but best appreciated from the vantage point of the opposite pavement. Long neglected, the building has a remarkable iron-framed interior.

The **Grant Arms**

188 Argyle Street, G2
0141 229 5831

A pub with an interesting history. The original tavern on this site dated back to 1834. Under early proprietor Walter Gibson, it was established as 'the original home of the welsh rarebit' in Glasgow. In the late 19th century it was acquired by Mathew Paxton, who maintained the old chop house traditions, but remodelled the premises in time for the opening of the 1888 Glasgow Exhibition. In the early 1900s, Paxton's was bought by Finlay Stuart Bell, of Chrystal, Bell & Co. An island bar was installed and the bar-room walls were adorned with valuable paintings. In the cellar were two huge vats containing the proprietor's own blended whiskies – 'Special Old Glen' and 'The Original No 4'.

In the 1930s, John Grant refurbished the premises in art deco style. His other catering enterprises included The Buchanan Arms hotel, Drymen. Notwithstanding these distinguished antecedents, the present lounge bar is of no particular interest, though the pub's central location has ensured popularity as a place for quick drinks and inexpensive lunches. Stuart Bell's art nouveau façade survives, designed by J H Craigie of Clarke and Bell.

The Grant Arms is adjacent to the 'Hielanman's Umbrella' – a huge railway bridge carrying elevated lines over the River Clyde to Central Station. This massive iron and glass structure splits Argyle Street into two contrasting halves. The pavements under the bridge were used as a Sunday meeting place by migrants from the Highlands and Islands.

The **Griffin**

266 Bath Street, G2
0141 331 5171

In 1903, spirit merchant Duncan Tweedley built this extravagant pub to attract theatre-goers. He called it The King's Arms, after the

nearby King's Theatre which was then under construction. Tweedley's new pub was designed by William Reid, a 'Glasgow Style' architect who specialised in bars. While the superb timber frontage is substantially intact, the original cut-glass windows have gone – though the present etched windows copy the art nouveau pattern. This distinguished pub has undergone numerous 'improvements' over the years – the last in 1999. Surviving Edwardian features include a U-shaped bar and moulded ceiling. The lounge/diners – The Griffiny and Griffinette – are, needless to say, modern additions. Inexpensive bar meals and snacks. Regular DJs. Live music sessions.

Bath Street takes its name from 'fine stretching baths' for ladies and gentlemen on the site of the present street. They were opened by William Harley, a 19th-century manufacturer and entrepreneur who sold water from his Willowbank estate at a halfpenny a 'stoup'. Harley opened a 'pleasure garden' on Blythswood Hill, and ran a model dairy, which had 100 cows. The fame of 'Harley's Byres' spread through Europe, and even attracted the attention of the Empress of Russia. Invited to St Petersburg to establish a similar facility, Harley died en route in London, in 1829.

The **Hengler's Circus**

352 Sauchiehall Street, G2
0141 332 8205

Formerly Shenanigan's, and since 2001 a J D Wetherspoon pub, The Hengler's Circus has little discernible character, though it has already built up a loyal clientele. As with other Wetherspoon outlets nationwide, real ales and good value meals and snacks are served, and there's a ban on music.

For twenty years, from 1904 to 1924, Hengler's Sauchiehall Street Circus was a Glasgow institution. The grand finale was usually a magnificent water pageant, one of the most popular of which was 'The Redskin', in which braves in canoes went over 'a cataract of real water'. The circus arena was lowered by hydraulic power and flooded to a depth of about ten feet. Between circus seasons, the Hengler family used the premises as a cinema. Hengler's Circus stood east of the present pub, at 326 Sauchiehall Street. The building was remodelled and reopened as the Waldorf Palais de Danse in 1927. Two years later it was rebuilt as the ABC Regal cinema. Currently lying empty, the building was last used as an MGM cinema. The site has figured hugely in popular culture, having housed dioramas, panoramas, an ice skating palace, a hippodrome, a circus, a dance hall, and several cinemas.

Henry's Café Bar

35 St Vincent Place, G1
0141 204 5240

Housed in what used to be Glasgow's tourist centre, and situated in one of the city's most impressive late-Victorian palaces of commerce, formerly the Scottish Amicable Building, this pub was opened in 1999 as the first Scottish link in the well-known chain of Henry's Café Bars, owned by Warrington-based Greenalls. The split-level interior, suggestive of *belle époque* styling, is devoid of local associations as befits a 'branded' pub chain with similar premises in locations as far apart as Cardiff and Leeds. A good range of meals and snacks ensures popularity with shoppers, office workers and tourists. Extensive cocktail menu.

The **Horse Shoe** Bar

17 Drury Street, G2
0141 229 5711

In the 1880s, large pubs with island bars came into fashion. In Scotland the model for many pubs of this character was Glasgow's Horse Shoe Bar. The premises were already long-established before 1884, when they were taken over and remodelled by an enterprising bar-owner called John Scouller.

To facilitate quick service, spirit casks on the central gantry were placed on their sides, with taps at each end. On either side of the bar,

there was a sitting-room with leather-upholstered seats and a fireplace. Two fireplaces were situated at the rear of the pub, where the wall was decorated with mirrors. Tall gasoliers rose from the bar counter and branched into triple lamps. In 1888, the licensed trade press reported bar-owners travelling from Dundee, Aberdeen and Inverness to inspect Scouller's new premises.

In 1901, the year of Glasgow's second International Exhibition, the partitions between sitting-rooms and bar were removed. The counter was enlarged at the rear; it also lost its gasoliers, but gained a shelf carried on miniature columns. Scouller was a keen Volunteer cavalryman and the pub abounds in equestrian references – on mirrors, chimney pieces and capitals of pillars. There's even a statuette of a farrier.

By the early 1900s, the pub had become a Glasgow institution. Telegraphed market prices were posted for the benefit of businessmen. The house speciality was 'Lachie' whisky, sold from the wood. The Horse Shoe Bar has featured in *The Guinness Book of Records* as the longest continuous bar in the UK. Sadly, the superb dark-stained matchboarded ceiling can no longer be seen, having been covered over during refurbishment in the 1980s.

The tiled floor is another modern 'improvement'. The huge mirrors once reflected white-aproned and fiercely-moustached barmen.

Scouller's successor, John Y Whyte, literally left his mark – superimposing his initials on mirrors and incising them into woodwork. Two Union Flag pendants in stained glass are relics of another of Whyte's pubs, The Union Café – formerly in Union Street.

Now B listed, The Horse Shoe Bar is one of the city's most popular hostelries. Food and drink are good value. Basic lunches are served in the historic bar and a buffet is available upstairs in the neo-Victorian restaurant – which is also one of Glasgow's main karaoke venues.

The **Imperial**

6 Howard Street, G1
0141 221 8217

A small and well-patronised traditional Glasgow local with lots of character. There's a semicircular bar, elegant gantry and interesting stained glass. A handsome antique mirror, from the Glasgow workshop of Forrest and Son, advertises Schweppes Table

Waters. Features Saturday night nostalgic disco (50s-90s pop – 8pm till late).

At the end of the 19th century, there were innumerable 'Empire' and 'Imperial' bars and restaurants throughout the UK.

Howard Street, named after English prison reformer John Howard, was laid out in 1768 and was extended east from St Enoch Square in 1798.

Lauder's

76 Sauchiehall Street, G2
0141 331 5180

Not named after Sir Harry Lauder, as you might have thought. This was originally The Royal Lochnagar Vaults, owned by Archibald Lauder, a prominent and decidedly extrovert late-Victorian whisky merchant, who took his surname so seriously that he published a book entitled *The Family of Lauder*. In the late 1890s, this pub was immensely popular with theatre-goers, and it's still one of the most popular howffs in Sauchiehall Street. In its Victorian heyday, there were two bars: an island bar at the front and a semicircular bar at the rear. A model distillery was

exhibited in one of the windows. Lauder's 'Royal Northern Cream' won a gold medal at the Edinburgh Exhibition of 1886, and he took his blend of 'the cratur' to the 1893 Chicago World's Fair. He also exported whiskies to Russia. Another speciality of The Royal Lochnagar Vaults was Ten Guinea Ale, a brew of fearsome potency.

The late-Victorian pub interior was destroyed many years ago and after its most recent refurbishment, in 1995. Lauder's is a large, low-ceilinged split-level pub, with semicircular bar, pillared gantry, and old photographs with Scottish associations, including portraits of Sir Harry – but none of Archibald! Bar meals and snacks served Mon-Sat 12-7; Sun 12.30-5. À la carte menu available 4pm-7.30pm Mon-Sat.

Los Borrachos

2 St George's Road, G3

0141 332 7000

This informal Mexican-themed bar-restaurant, formerly known as The Corner and Speaker's Corner,

is situated in Charing Cross Mansions (1891), John James Burnet's exuberant *fin de siècle* version of French Renaissance architecture. The premises were originally an upmarket Edwardian shop. The menu here, as one would expect, features Mexican specialities, including tortillas, nachos, enchiladas, and burritos.

McConnell's

335 Hope Street, G2
0141 331 6021

An informal lounge bar, situated in a lavish neo-Baroque tenement, erected by the City Improvement Trust in 1906-7 at the Cowcaddens end of Hope Street. Inexpensive bar lunches. Handy for the Theatre Royal.

Maclachlan's Brew Bar

57 West Regent Street, G2
0141 332 0595

Opened in 2000, this unusual café-bar blends Pictish imagery with fragments from an original opulent Edwardian interior. Beer is brewed on the premises from 100% organic Scottish ingredients, and there's also a large selection of malts. The menu – also 100% organic – is imaginative and comparatively inexpensive. Live music every Sunday evening.

Castle Chambers, eight storeys in height, and built of red sandstone and pink granite, was completed in 1902 as the headquarters of brothers George and John Maclachlan, whose 'Castle' chain of pubs was an early example of 'pub branding'. The Maclachlans were brewers and distillers as well as wholesale and retail wine and spirit merchants. In the Edwardian period they exported to India and South Africa and supplied their 'Five Castle' whisky to the House of Lords. The Maclachlans used a castle as their trademark, and it survives, executed in mosaic, in the entrance to the present café-bar. The premises originally housed The Palace Restaurant, which rivalled The Grosvenor Restaurant as the haunt of the city's prosperous young Edwardians.

MacSorley's

42 Jamaica Street, G1
0141 572 0199

In the early 1890s an opulent pub called The Clan Vaults stood here. It was acquired by Philip MacSorley in 1897 and within two years a new commercial block was rising on the site.

MacSorley's splendid new pub, illuminated by electricity, opened in 1899. It had a large oval-shaped mahogany island bar and a much smaller snack and oyster counter. Within the main bar, the ornately carved gantry reached almost to the ceiling. Walls were partly panelled, partly stencilled, in avant-garde fashion. By 1903, there was an attractive dining room, in addition to a well-upholstered smoking-room, a suite of rooms for ladies, and an American cocktail bar – in the charge of a New York barman acquainted with the mysteries of Gin Slings, Mint Juleps and Corpse Revivers. In addition to owning a famous Manhattan bar (still in existence), Philip MacSorley owned several of Edwardian Glasgow's best-known pubs, including The Hampden Vaults, Crossmyloof, where he sold a special blend of whiskies called 'the Peacemaker'.

Elegant art nouveau exterior woodwork and richly embossed windows survive from the magnificent *fin de siècle* pub Munro knew. When the premises were refurbished in 2000 (after several previous lamentable refittings), contractors removed a false ceiling and revealed an elaborate original. MacSorley's now particularly welcomes gays. Open noon-midnight except Sun (12.30-midnight). Inexpensive bar meals. Live music at weekends. Karaoke every Tue, Fri, Sat and Sun.

The **Maltman**

59 Renfield Street, G2
0141 331 0299

In 1604, maltmen comprised 55 out of 661 craftsmen in Glasgow, and the town's Incorporation of Maltmen was founded the following year. Most maltmen were also brewers, in the Scottish tradition. Malt-making was confined to members of the craft. Their monopoly lasted until 1846. In 1665, the Incorporation of Maltmen rebuked member Robert Corss, who'd bad-mouthed a fellow craftsman by asserting: 'There is not ane honest maltman in all Glasgow, but a whein of false villane knaves.'

The present hostelry, an outpost of John Barras & Co., is on two levels and bears the neo-Victorian hallmarks of current 'branded pub' chains, with pedimented gantries and brilliant-cut glass screens. Meals and snacks are served all day.

Molly Malone's

224 Hope Street, G2
0141 332 2757

A cavernous split-level Irish theme pub, opened in 1995. It was actually built in Ireland, shipped across the Irish Sea in pieces, and re-assembled in what used to be a telephone exchange. In Ireland, even town pubs sold dry goods, such as tea and sugar and some also served as post offices. Inexpensive bar fare.

Live music seven nights a week. Happy hours 4.30pm-8.30pm weekdays.

Molly Malone 'wheel'd her wheel-barrow thro' streets broad and narrow, crying, cockles and mussels! Alive, alive, O!' Poor Molly died of a fever, but her ghost continued to cry 'cockles and mussels!'

through the streets of Dublin in the wee small hours (no noise abatement orders in those days).

Montrose Bar and Diner

7 Carrick Street, G2
0141 572 0003

An oasis just off the Broomielaw, much frequented at lunchtime by office workers and journalists on parole from *The Daily Record* and *Sunday Mail*. In the bar, where the decor includes pictures of the Broomielaw (Glasgow Bridge Quay) when it was a thriving port, light snacks are served, while the diner, decorated in pseudo-Mackintosh style, offers an inexpensive and varied menu. There's also a beer garden for alfresco recreation on balmy summer days – by no means unknown in the dear green place.

Nico's

379 Sauchiehall Street, G2
0141 332 5736

Informal brasserie-style café-bar, one of the first continental-style hostelries in the city, and now over 21 years old. There's a long curved bar in the front half of the premises, where the walls are decorated with tiles and mirrors. *Belle époque* influence can also be seen in the back half, where the walls are adorned with murals depicting voluptuous *fin de siècle* damsels. Menu ranges from all-day brunch to speciality dishes. DJs Thu-Sun. Daily drinks promotions.

O'Henry's

14 Drury Street, G1
0141 248 3751

Upstairs at O'Henry's, there's a split-level café-bar.

Downstairs, a candle-lit wine cellar. Varied café-style lunch menu. DJs at weekends.

Drury Street joins West Nile Street with Union Street. It was originally called West Nile Lane. As late as 1848, sedan chairs could be hired at 21 Drury Street.

O'Neill's

155 Queen Street, G11
0141 229 5871

One of a chain of Irish theme bars opened in the 1990s, this pub offers friendly service and tasty meals and snacks. Handy for the Gallery of Modern Art.

Glasgow's second Theatre Royal was opened on this site in 1805. On 18 September 1818, when the theatre's 'grand crystal lustre' was illuminated for the first time with 'sparkling gas', crowds flocked to witness the

phenomenon. Some of the finest Thespians of the day trod the boards of the Queen Street Theatre Royal, but 'sparkling gas', via a leaky pipe joint, was the theatre's undoing. It burnt down in January 1829.

Ocho

150 West Campbell Street, G2
0141 332 1032

Formerly known as The Whisky Bar, this hostelry has the misfortune to be attached to the Sauchiehall Centre, an aesthetic blight built in the 1970s on the site of Pettigrew and Stephens' magnificent late-Victorian department store, The Manchester House. The varied menu is much appreciated by shoppers and office workers. Tuesday 'student night' spirits promos.

There were once several grand Victorian pubs in this vicinity. The Metropolitan Bar (164 Sauchiehall Street) had a sumptuous sitting-room with marble-lined walls and was patronised by the town's 'mashers' – trendy young men who wore tight trousers, short jackets, high collars, and boots with pointed toes.

Oko

68 Ingram Street, G1
0141 572 1500

The minimalist Oko bar, located on the mezzanine above a Japanese restaurant, is as good a place as any to sample beers from the land of the rising sun. DJs most weekends.

Old Empire Bar

66 Saltmarket, G1
0141 552 0844

There has been a tavern on this site since at least the 1840s. Now a friendly nondescript traditional local.

Old Printworks

38 North Frederick Street, G1
0141 552 8160

This unusual split-level pub was formerly the premises of and old-established city printers, William Hodge & Company. The original 'wally tiled' stairwell has been preserved. The Old Printworks adjoins George

Square and is handy for Queen Street station and the Buchanan Galleries, the area's premier shopping centre. As is characteristic of Hogshead establishments the ales are served in excellent condition and service is efficient and courteous. Inexpensive meals and snacks served Sun-Thur until 9pm; Fri-Sat until 8pm.

The **Old Ship Bank Tavern**

164 Saltmarket, G1
0141 552 7705

There has been a Ship Bank Tavern on this site for well over a century. This one is a friendly, untrendy local, opened in 1904. There's no trace of the original 'Glasgow Style' island bar, which was divided into semi-private spaces by stained glass partitions.

The tenement in which the pub is situated occupies the site of the Ship Bank, Glasgow's first bank. Robert Carrick, manager of the Ship Bank, was a notorious skinflint. When he died at the age of 81, he left a fortune. Bank security in olden times was rudimentary. The youngest apprentice had to guard the Ship Bank at night. He was provided with a gun and bugle and locked in until morning. The Ship Bank was later absorbed by the Glasgow Union Bank, which in 1843 became the Union Bank of Scotland.

Pitcher and Piano

92 West George Street, G2
0141 353 3003

Occupying the former banking hall of James Miller's Commercial Bank (1930-7), this attractive café-bar is yet another successful listed building conversion. Lofty windows, enriched with art deco ironwork, provide impressive glimpses of central Glasgow's palaces of commerce. Good lunch venue. Varied menu served all day from noon until midnight. After WW1 the neo-classical style – with art deco trimmings – became increasingly associated with banks, insurance offices and corporate headquarters. With their impressive rows of Graeco-Roman columns, these giant buildings earned the uncomplimentary epithet 'temples of Mammon'.

The **Press Bar**

199 Albion Street, G1
0141 552 5142

Cheerful cosy lounge bar, traditional haunt of press hacks. Inexpensive bar snacks.

The largest and oldest portion of the former Caledonian Newspapers building, fronting Albion Street, was originally occupied by The Scottish Daily Express. Like its Fleet Street counterpart – the so-called 'Black Lubyanka' – it was designed by Sir E Owen Williams and is an impressive 'streamlined' *art moderne* composition in alternating glass windows and shiny black vitrolite.

RG's

73 Queen Street, G1
0141 221 2200

This was originally Lang's Restaurant, a famous Victorian fast food establishment which was revamped in the 1930s in *art moderne* style. In 1978, Lang's became a trendy pub known as The Rock Garden. Retaining the pre-war restaurant's faience exterior, this split-level bar has also preserved a few art deco touches, including stylish lighting pendants. Good choice of bar food, served noon-5.45 Sun-Wed; noon-7.45 Thur-Sat. Drinks promos. Regular DJs.

William Lang, 'the Napoleon of sandwiches', pioneered self-service catering. In the 1880s, around 200 varieties of sandwiches were on offer in his Queen Street 'quick lunch bar', including lobster, grouse, blackcock, partridge, and pheasant. Patrons drew their own supplies of claret, whisky, ale or porter from small casks, stillioned on the bar. Everyone was obliged to eat and drink standing up. Lang operated an 'honour system', trusting his customers to personally itemise all the food and drink they consumed.

The **Renfield Bar**

70 Renfield Street
0141 332 1842

Opened in 1995 as Jock Tamson's, a nostalgic 'Highland bothy' pub with matchboarded walls and ceiling, stone fireplace, and portraits of Highland worthies. Inexpensive bar meals.

Republic Bier Halle

9 Gordon Street
0141 204 0706

Nothing could be less like a lofty and cavernous Teutonic beer hall than this inobtrusive basement bar. More than 100 beers from around the world are on offer here, along with a wide range of cocktails, vodkas and schnapps and four brands of absinthe! Appetising snacks and meals are served from midday until 7pm, and service is attentive and friendly. Happy hours, 5-7 Mon-Fri. Live music from top DJs.

Gordon Street was laid out in 1802 by Alexander Gordon, a wealthy West India merchant, known as 'Picture Gordon' on account of his art collection. When he moved to London, his Buchanan Street mansion was demolished and the Royal Bank of Scotland HQ (now Borders bookshop) was erected on the site. The Ca'd'Oro building, at the south-west corner of Gordon Street and Union Street, a magnificent cast-iron building of the 1870s, was restored in 1989 after a major fire. In the 1920s the building housed The Ca'd'Oro Restaurant, Glasgow's smartest functions venue, with decor inspired by the palaces and canals of Venice.

The **Rogano**

11 Exchange Place, G1
0141 248 4055

In the early 1870s the London-based Bodega Company opened a branch in Exchange Place. When they withdrew from Glasgow, the business was taken over by their manager, James Roger, who traded under the name Rogano Ltd. By 1913, when Roger died, there were also Rogano establishments in North Street, New City Road, Kilmarnock Road and Paisley Road. The speciality of the firm was Spanish wines, drawn straight from the wood, but by WW1 Rogano bars were also selling the 'Colonel Bogey' blend of whisky.

In 1935, the Exchange

Place branch was refurbished as a seafood restaurant, modelled on the smart Prunier restaurants in Paris and London. Architects Weddell and Inglis used bright yellow vitrolite for the exterior and part of the premises served as a wine shop. The Rogano is now a 'must see' for all fans of upmarket art deco. On the ground floor, the original deco front bar dispenses champagne cocktails, while the adjoining restaurant, also pukka 1930s, specialises in Scottish seafood. Eating in the restaurant can seriously damage your bank balance but comparatively inexpensive lunches are served downstairs in the Café Rogano, a modern addition.

Ross's

78 Mitchell Street, G1
0141 229 5881

Formerly this hostelry was called The Gordon Bar. The original owner, David Ross, made money from cattle dealing and gold mining in Australia and New Zealand. In the 1890s, The Gordon Bar was an upmarket late-Victorian 'palace pub' and the facilities included a telephone room. In 1903, however, Ross commissioned Gordon Chambers, an eight-storey (including basement) Edwardian Baroque mercantile building. In the course of construction, the proprietor's initials and the date 1905 were inscribed on the principal, Mitchell Street, façade. The old pub was demolished, but the new Gordon Bar was a worthy replacement.

Exterior granite, ornamental ironwork and etched glass survive from the second Gordon Bar, but internally, the present pub is merely a pastiche of Edwardian 'palace pub' style, with a better than average long bar and gantry. Inexpensive bar meals.

Sadie Frost's

8-10 West George Street, G1
0141 332 8005

Big upmarket gay venue with separate lesbians-only bar. Open daily noon-midnight.

The Scotia Bar

112 Stockwell Street, G1
0141 552 8681

This much-loved howff, dates from 1929, when it was known as Ye Olde Scotia Bar. At that time there was a

vogue for mock-Tudor pubs (there was a second 'Tudor' craze in the 1960s). The intimate atmosphere is helped by a low-beamed ceiling and dark wall panelling. There's an extensive collection of old Glasgow photographs and a cosy wood-panelled snug. The Scotia has starred in episodes of *Taggart*. Traditional Scottish music sessions are a feature of this outstanding example of echt Glaswegian pub culture. Inexpensive bar lunches.

The Scotia Bar perpetuates the memory of the old Scotia Music Hall, opened by James Bayliss in 1862. It was unlicensed until 1892. Performers who trod the boards included Dan Leno, Marie Lloyd, Little Tich, Vesta Tilley, and George Leybourne, the original 'Champagne Charlie'. In 1875, The Scotia presented 'Sidney and Alphonse the marvellous child velocipedists' and 'La Petite Robina the wonderful child actress'.

In 1896, The Scotia was renamed The Metropole, a theatre specialising in melodramas such as 'A Woman Adrift' and 'From Mill Girl To Millionaire'. By 1901, The Metropole was a variety theatre, and it was there that Harry Lauder made his professional debut. It was destroyed by fire in 1961.

70s Revival Bar – Flares

73 Bath Street, G2

Previously known as Phileas Fogg, this is a split-level basement bar/diner with low ceilings and nostalgia for 'the Purple Decade'. You'll be sorry you shaved off your droopy Mexican-bandit moustache and gave your aviator sunglasses, flared trousers, kipper ties and platform boots to Oxfam.

Sloan's

62 Argyle Arcade, G2
0141 221 8917

In 1900, David Sloan opened The Arcade Café, consisting of richly furnished dining rooms, private supper rooms, and bars. Several years later, the proprietor added a 'cigar divan'. In 1906, a banqueting hall was added to the amenities. The public bar here has lost its original opulent character, but much *fin de siècle* and Edwardian decoration survives upstairs in the restaurant, banqueting hall and private supper rooms. There's lots of virtuoso embossed glass, and the vestibule leading from the Arcade is richly tiled. Good value bar menu.

Slug and Lettuce

23-25 St Vincent Place, G1
0141 243 2402

Cavernous minimalist designer bar, an outlet of the English-based Slug and Lettuce chain, opened in 1998 in the basement and ground floor of the imposing grade A

listed Scottish Provident Building (1904-8). Popular with city office workers and trendy young professionals. Varied menu available from opening time until 9pm.

Soba

11 Mitchell Lane, G1
0141 204 2404

Coctails are a big thing in this trendy bar, located next

to the Lighthouse, opened in 1999 as an exhibition venue for architecture and design. The location is the former Glasgow Herald building (1895), Charles Rennie Mackintosh's first public commission. In addition to mounting temporary exhibitions, The Lighthouse houses The Mackintosh Interpretation Centre, a permanent exhibition space devoted to the work of Glasgow's most famous son.

The **State Bar**

148 Holland Street, G2
0141 332 2159

David Sloan, of the sumptuous Arcade Café, opened this pub in 1906. The handsome Edwardian interior survived until the1960s. The State Bar is now a real ale theme bar, with a stylish neo-Victorian island bar. During alterations, a window with heraldic stained glass, a relic of Sloan's original pub, was discovered behind interior brickwork and has been retained. Regular and guest ales are on tap in this friendly, well-run establishment, which is open Mon-Sat 11am until midnight (Sun 12.30pm-midnight).

The **Station Bar**

55 Port Dundas Road, G4
0141 332 3117

A well-run friendly bar/lounge, convenient for the Theatre Royal and Sauchiehall Street. It takes its name from Buchanan Street railway station (closed 1966). Three well-kept cask-conditioned ales are on tap, and a traditional informal Glasgow pub culture pervades. The Station Bar was formerly an Edwardian pub, with perforated bench seats to facilitate the beneficial effects of a state-of-the-art heating system. The bar still exhibits an antique mirror advertising McEwan's Pale Ale.

Times Square

48 St Enoch Square, G1
0141 221 6579

Informal and unpretentious bar/diner, on the opposite side of the Square from the giant St Enoch Centre shopping mall (1981-89), and hence a popular lunch venue.

Inexpensive bar food served noon-5.30pm. Full menu Sun-Thur 3-5.30; Fri-Sat 5-7.30. Drinks promos Thur-Fri-Sat 6pm-midnight.

Toby Jug

8 Waterloo Street, G2
0141 221 4159

Popular split-level real ale lounge bar, handy for Central Station. In 1887, this long-established pub, formerly known as The Blythswood Bar, was described as being 'situated in a quiet, out of the way thoroughfare'. Construction of the Central Station Hotel in 1884 helped to turn Hope Street into a major traffic artery. By the early 1890s, The Blythswood Bar consisted of a large bar and dining room. The proprietor, like many of his peers, exhibited curios to attract custom. The pride of his collection was an ornate snuff mull, allegedly made out of the left hind hoof of Tam o' Shanter's grey mare Meg. By Edwardian times, the pub was a great favourite with the mercantile community – the city's Corn Exchange (now demolished) was in the immediate vicinity.

The Tolbooth Bar

11 Saltmarket, G1
0141 572 0531

Opened in 1908 as The Coat of Arms. In Edwardian times, when Glasgow Cross was very rough, especially on Saturday nights, a smartly uniformed commissionaire acted as bouncer. Much original character has been lost, but some virtuoso engraved glass, an unspoilt example of a richly modelled Edwardian gantry, and traditional Glasgow pub atmosphere, make the present bar well worth a visit. Live Irish folk sessions.

The Tolbooth Bar takes its name from the seven-storey steeple at the foot of the High Street, the only surviving portion of the Tolbooth, built in the 1620s, Gothicised in the early 1800s, and torn down in 1921. The earliest

'tolbooth' was where tolls payable by those bringing produce to market were collected. Originally, iron spikes, reserved for the heads and dismembered limbs of traitors and 'papists', protruded from the present steeple. In the 'great fire' of 1677, the Tolbooth clock was destroyed by the fierce heat, but the building itself was undamaged.

Trader Joe's

325 Hope Street, G2
0141 353 3236

Friendly informal 1990s theme bar with a lively young clientele. Drinks promos, regular DJs and karaoke. Bar snacks and meals, including burgers, grills and Scottish specialities, served noon till 7.30pm Mon-Sat.

The Theatre Royal, opposite, moved to Hope Street from Dundas Street in 1869. The present theatre, the third on the site, was built in 1895 by C J Phipps. In the early 1900s, the area from the top of Hope Street down to Sauchiehall Street was 'the Soho of Glasgow', inhabited by Italian barbers, theatrical costumiers, and vendors of pornographic photographs.

The **Vale**

5 Dundas Street, G1
0141 333 0946

As the years go by, there are fewer and fewer pubs in Glasgow with historic roots. This pub, however, has such antecedents. Originally opened in 1891, and named after the Vale of Leven, a popular amateur football team of the period, it had a fashionable circular bar with central gantry supporting whisky barrels. There was also a new-fangled telephone,

and football results were phoned to the pub every Saturday. The present establishment largely dates from the 1930s and, when it was in pristine condition, featured an upstairs cocktail bar, with an angular art deco counter and mirror in etched peach glass. Handy for Queen Street station.

The **Variety Bar**

401 Sauchiehall Street, G2
0141 332 4449

In the 1970s, when theme bars were the height of fashion, this was The Norsk

Inn. The original Variety Bar was situated at 15 Cowcaddens Street. The present bar dates from the late 1980s and the exterior is 1930s pastiche – a simplified version of the old Variety Bar's vitrolite frontage, which was decorated with pictures of variety artists, including Sir Harry Lauder. Inside, there's a chrome-banded 'streamlined' counter, with repro art deco lights and wall freize. Located opposite Strathclyde University's Baird Hall of Residence, formerly the Beresford Hotel (1938), The Variety Bar is popular with students. DJs six nights a week. Daily happy hours 11am-8pm. Inexpensive bar snacks.

The **Victoria Bar**

159 Bridgegate, G1
0141 552 6040

This pub is a local institution, long renowned for live folk music and an inimitable authentic Glasgow pub atmosphere – something which can't be reproduced by any amount of expensive pub 'branding' or 'styling'. Dark-stained matchboard walls and ceiling contribute to the character of the original

Victorian public bar, where the gantry is adorned with a mirror advertising Robert Younger's extinct St Ann's Brewery. Traditional Scottish bar snacks such as bridies are supplied by Flemings of Arbroath, and well-kept real ales are dispensed from antique brass fonts.

Vivo

97-103 West George Street, G1
0141 226 2441

Like All Bar One, this trendy café/bar disassociates itself from the city's masculine pub traditions. Behind the shop-like glass frontage, there's lots of stripped pine and bright colours. Like many of Glasgow's current wave of bars, this is a popular pre-club venue at weekends. A varied menu and salsa dance lessons are also available here. Resident DJ.

Vroni's

47 West Nile Street, G1
0141 221 4677

Smith's, the previous bar at this address, sold in excess of 25 wines. Its successor, Vroni's, opened in 1995, has over 100 wines on offer, with ten varieties sold by the glass. Decor is low-key and pleasant. Champagne happy hour on Saturday nights. Lunch menu.

The Waterloo Bar

306 Argyle Street, G2
0141 229 5891

Long-established as a gay pub, and believed to be the oldest such pub in Scotland. In bygone days, when the gay scene was 'underground', gay pubs had to be inobtrusive. They were often situated in the vicinity of theatres and music halls. The Waterloo Bar

was originally a 'theatrical' pub, catering for artists and groupies from the nearby Alhambra Theatre, and it may well have been a covertly gay venue before WW1, as were many similar pubs in that era. When owned by David Ross, this was one of Glasgow's finest Edwardian 'palace pubs'. The customers' side of the long bar was broken up by shallow screens of ornate design. The present decor is largely a pastiche of Edwardian style. Open Mon-Sat noon-midnight, Sun 12.30pm-midnight.

Waxy O'Conner's

46 West George Street, G1
0141 354 5154

Labyrinthine, extravagantly themed 'Irish' pub, handy for the Buchanan Galleries shopping centre and Queen Street station. There are six bars on different levels (including the obligatory 'Irish' bar-cum-shop). The largest, the Church Bar, features pulpit, organ, and upholstered pews. More intimate spaces, such as the Library Bar and the Cottage Lounge, are well suited to eating and drinking tête-à-tête. Meals and snacks are appetising, and the service is friendly.

Yates Wine Lodge

136 West George Street, G2
0141 353 3926

Traditional ostentatious bar fittings, bevelled and brilliant-cut mirrors, and heavy coffered ceilings are features of this busy split-level Yates Brothers hostelry, housed in a Victorian palazzo, originally built for the Clydesdale Bank. Food served 11am till 7pm. Drinks promos 2pm-8pm daily. Late night menu Mon-Thur 5-10pm.

This district – lying west of High Street and north of Trongate – contains most of the city's pre-Victorian buildings. It was Glasgow's first 'new town', laid out on a gridiron plan, later adopted by many American cities. Construction began in the mid-1780s with Brunswick Street, Hutcheson Street and Wilson Street. As a residential quarter, the 'new town' lasted barely three decades and by the 1820s it was occupied largely by the expanding textile industry. Wealthy merchants moved to a second 'new town', set in splendid isolation on Blythswood Hill. When that also fell to commercial pressures, they pursued their relentless *Drang nach Westen* to the limits of the present west end at Anniesland. Since the 1980s, the original Georgian development has been the focus of some exemplary conservation work. In 1989 Glasgow won a Europa Nostra Medal of Honour for the Merchant City regeneration.

While the term 'Merchant City' refers specifically to the Georgian 'new town', a number of interesting pubs are situated in the immediate vicinity of the 'new town' – south of Glasgow Cross, in the Saltmarket, Bridgegate and Stockwell area, which was Glasgow's oldest centre of mercantile activity. These pubs can be found in the City Centre section.

Arta

13 Walls Street, G1
0141 552 2101

Opened in 2000, this stylish transformation of the old Corporation Cheese Market consists of three bars, a restaurant and a club. An uninviting exterior does little to prepare punters for the delights within. Cavernous candlelit main bar oozes atmosphere and features a Mediterranean-style courtyard with abundant ornamental features. Restaurant upstairs. Function rooms available for private hire Wed-Sun. Comedy, cabaret and live music 9pm till late every Thur, Fri and Sat in basement venue.

Babbity Bowster

16 Blackfriars Street, G1
0141 552 5055

Opened in 1986, this celebrated hotel/pub /restaurant is named after an old Scottish country dance which used to round off a ball or wedding celebration. Situated in an elegant late-Georgian warehouse, designed by James Adam, Babbity Bowster is one of the Merchant City's most popular hostelries. In the bar, the shades-of-grey colour scheme and plastic finishes may be contemporary touches, but the painted ceiling beams and open fire are reflections of older traditions. A ceramic panel depicts a kilted Scot dancing the 'Babbity Bowster' – or 'Bab at the Bowster' (a bowster is a bolster or pillow). Several well-kept cask-conditioned ales

available in the bar, which opens at 8am for breakfast every day and serves a full menu (including Scottish specialities such as stovies and haggis) from noon until midnight. Upstairs the restaurant offers a more extensive menu. A small beer garden makes this pub specially attractive on hot summer days. Regular fiddle music in the bar.

Bargo

80 Albion Street, G1
0141 553 4771

Vast brewery-owned 'style bar', opened in the mid-1990s. Popular with students from nearby University of Strathclyde.

DJs at weekends. Regular student drink promos. Good value bar meals.

Bar 91

91 Candleriggs, G1
0141 552 5211

Now well-established, this trendy pub was a pioneering Merchant City 'style bar'. DJs at weekends. Restaurant upstairs. Sunday brunch menu. Happy hours 5-8pm.

In the 18th century, the 'soaperie' or soap factory established by the Whale-fishing Company stood opposite here, at the corner of Candleriggs and Back Cow Loan (Ingram Street).

In the early 19th century, The Ramshorn Tavern stood in this vicinity. It took its name from the original Ramshorn Church. The present church is the second on the Ingram Street site. Supposedly, it got its unusual name because St Mungo performed a miracle there, turning a stolen ram's head into stone. When Ingram Street – originally a country lane – was widened, part of Ramshorn burying ground was sacrificed, and the initials R F and A F on the pavement outside the church mark the graves of Robert and Andrew Foulis, who earned a European reputation as printers of fine books, including folio editions of Homer's *Iliad* and *Odyssey*. The Foulis brothers also

established an Academy of Fine Arts, 15 years before London's Royal Academy was founded.

Blackfriars

36 Bell Street, G1
0141 552 5924

Informal bistro-style pub, now a local institution. Good value bar meals make it popular with students and Merchant City workers and residents. Well-kept real ales. Live music at weekends. Sunday night comedy club downstairs.

In the 18th century, Bell's Wynd (as it was then called) had many prosperous residents, and the richly sculptured 'port', or gateway, at the Wynd's entrance was a much-admired landmark.

The Blane Valley

76 Glassford Street, G1
0141 552 4286

As late as 1931, when Tennent's 90/- ale was on draught, this pub was still called by its original name: The Blane Valley Spirit Stores. On the ground floor of an early 19th-century warehouse, it originally belonged to whisky merchants Peter Buchanan and James Scott. Their cipher is still above the doors. Designed by Frank Burnet, an architect responsible for some of Glasgow's earliest 'palace pubs', it opened in 1887. The pub was advantageously sited, opposite Robert Adam's handsome Trades House (1791-94), the regular meeting place of the 14 Incorporated Trades of Glasgow. There used to be 15 until the Surgeons decided that they were too superior to rank as tradesmen!

In its pristine state, when house specialities included 1858 brandy and 1870 Jamaica rum, The Blane Valley had a decor similar to The Horse Shoe Bar in Drury Street. The bar was in the form of an elongated 'U', with

a richly carved gantry in the middle supporting spirit casks. The rear wall was decorated with mirrors and pilasters. There were three snugs, glazed with stained glass in floral designs. In the 1890s, customers could help themselves to free snacks of biscuits and cheese: New York bars of the 1880s were celebrated for a lavish provision of free snacks, and by the following decade enterprising Glasgow bar-owners had introduced the American 'free lunch' system. While the handsome arcaded frontage of The Blane Valley has survived, the interior has been remodelled and lacks the old pub's opulent late-Victorian character. Inexpensive bar menu served Mon-Sat 12-7; Sun 12.30-4.30.

Café **Delmonica's**

68 Virginia Street, G1
0141 552 4803

Trendy, very popular gay café-bar in an imposing mercantile building. Open daily noon-midnight. Good value menu. DJs most weekday nights. Quiz on Thu and karaoke on Sun. Fri and Sat nights are reserved for dancing. Happy hours noon-2pm, 5-7pm and 9-10pm Mon-Sat and noon-7pm Sun.

In the mid-18th century, tobacco merchant Andrew Buchanan purchased a number of fields and vegetable gardens here. His son George built the Virginia Mansion, which stood at the north end of the present

street. Like its neighbour, the Shawfield Mansion, it was a handsome Palladian building and its ornamental gardens stretched north to Back Cow Loan (Ingram Street). George Buchanan also developed the approach to the house as a street.

The Glasgow Highland Society bought a plot at the south-east corner of Virginia Street (now occupied by Marks and Spencer's store) and built The Black Bull Inn, for the entertainment of Highlanders. In 1759, the new hostelry claimed that 'Great care has been taken to keep the bed-rooms at a distance from the drinking-rooms'. A famous Glasgow club, the Beggar's Benison, held their meetings in The Black Bull, and Robert Burns stayed there twice, in 1787 and 1788.

Cairns

7 Miller Street, G1
0141 248 5007

In the 1890s, Robert Cairns owned four Glasgow pubs. He was assisted in business by his brothers David and Alexander. This hostelry was a typical late-Victorian 'palace pub', where newspapers and

periodicals were provided for the patrons, who, comfortably ensconced in snugs, rang electric bells for attention. The speciality of the house was William Younger's Edinburgh Ale.

The original interior no longer exists but the present pub's open-plan character is enhanced by a low ceiling and a circular bar. Inexpensive bar food is served all day, with a separate evening menu.

Chambers

57 Cochrane Street, G1
0141 552 1740

Formerly The Queen's Bar, this pub was refurbished in the early 1990s in 'smuggler's inn' fashion, with a long bar, bare plank floors, low ceilings, and the usual nicotine-yellow walls. Regular drinks promos. Food served 12.30pm-9pm.

The pub takes its name from the City Chambers directly opposite, built between 1882-90 by London Scot William Young, who described his grandiose creation as 'a free and dignified treatment of the

Italian renaissance'. When the foundation stone was laid in 1883, Glasgow was *en fête*, with colourful processions of the Incorporated Trades. Though clad with freestone, some 10 million bricks were used in the building's construction. The interiors, encrusted with marble, alabaster, faience and mosaic, are magnificent (in a recent movie, *The House of Mirth*, they were used to convey the opulence of millionaire palaces in 1900s New York). The banqueting hall contains paintings and decoration by 'Glasgow Boys' such as John Lavery, Alexander Roche, and Edward Walton.

The **Court Bar**

69 Hutcheson Street, G1
0141 552 2463

Wall panelling and peach mirror glass gives the interior of this bijou pub a 1950s feeling, though it's probably later. Functions as gay venue in the evenings. Popular with leather crowd, particularly at weekends. Open Mon-Sat 8am-midnight, Sun 12.30pm-midnight.

The Court Bar sits opposite the west façade of the former County Buildings and Courthouses, a vast Greek Revival pile, originally built by Clarke and Bell in 1841, and subsequently enlarged and remodelled.

Fiddler's Court

49 Bell Street, G1
0141 552 3539

A giant stylised clock behind the bar and eccentric carriage

lamps, which may have strayed here from a defunct Venetian trattoria, are the only notable features in this small, low-ceilinged hostelry, popular with students, office workers and other Merchant City types. Inexpensive meals and snacks available 11.45-5.30 Mon-Sat; 12.30-4.45 Sun.

By the mid-19th century, some closes in the vicinity of High Street were a byword for squalor. The one with the worst reputation was Fiddler's Close (75 High Street). It was swept away by the City Improvement Trust in 1878. In its heyday, Fiddler's Close had been highly respectable. It reputedly took its name from the large numbers of musicians who lived there during the prosperous days of the 18th century.

Fix

86 Miller Street, G1
0141 221 1568

Large, split-level, semi-basement café-bar. Families are welcome. The windows afford an unusual worm's-eye view of some of Glasgow's finest Victorian warehouses, now converted into flats. Food served till 7pm Mon-Wed; till 8pm Thur-Fri; Sun 12.30-5.30.

Miller Street was laid out in 1762 for John Miller of Westerton, who had a brewery at Grahamston. When he feued his garden as a new street, he had to pull down one half of his house (he continued to live in the other half). Miller Street was originally a street of detached villas, all of which had gardens behind them. The

street's last 18th-century house, at number 42, dates from 1775 and has been restored by the Glasgow Building Preservation Trust.

Granny Black's

55 Candleriggs, G1
0141 552 2470

In the early 1890s, this pub was known as The Stag Vaults. It was one of the first Glasgow pubs to be equipped with an island bar, oval in shape, with a central gantry supporting whisky barrels. Side walls were hung with huge mirrors emblazoned with stags. The 'Stag Blend' of whisky was sold from the barrel, at 10d per gill. This friendly, well-run pub serves good-value food – including traditional mince and tatties – Mon-Sat noon till 4pm; Sun 12.30 till 4. 'Ye Olde' decor includes flock wallpaper and horse brasses.

The original Granny Black is supposed to have sold sixpenny teas in Glasgow's east end and specialised in twopenny mutton pies. Late-Victorian pie lovers flocked to 'Pie Smith's', a restaurant at the corner of Argyle Street and Maxwell Street.

Kilkenny's

17 John Street, G1
0141 552 3505

Subterranean Irish theme bar, frequented by students from nearby seats of learning. Cheap bar food. DJs most nights. Large screen TV and several pool tables.

McChuill's

40 High Street, G1
0141 552 2135

Trendy bar/restaurant, located in atmospheric railway arches behind a huge Victorian warehouse, built for the Glasgow & South-Western Railway, and converted into flats in the 1980s. Happy hours: 5-7pm daily. Regular DJs and live bands at weekends. Rotating menu

offering Scottish and cosmopolitan fare at reasonable prices.

The **Mitre Bar**

12 Brunswick Street, G1
0141 552 3764

An unobtrusive friendly little local, full of character. Bar counter and gantry are of sub-art nouveau pattern. The upstairs lounge/diner is plain but comfortable. Inexpensive bar meals and well-kept real ale.

In the early 19th century, a prestigious tavern, called The Prince of Wales, stood at 33 Brunswick Street. There, the Medical Club, composed of leading members of the Faculty of Physicians and Surgeons, held their monthly socials. The street owes its name to a sycophantic 18th-century habit of calling new streets after the Hanoverian Royal Family. It honours George IV's wife Caroline, a Princess of Brunswick.

Nearby, at 115 Trongate, there's the Italianate façade of Scotland's earliest music hall, The Britannia (1857) – which started life as Campbell's Music Saloon. It closed in 1903 but was reopened as The Panopticon, a 'rough' hall where the patrons did not suffer mediocre 'turns' with equanimity. Friday nights

were 'amateur nights', when hapless performers were pelted with rotten fruit, or hauled off by the manager wielding a shepherd's crook. Now a grade A listed building, the old 'Brit' retains its original proscenium and galleries and awaits restoration when funds permit.

In the 1890s, the Old Wynd, a few yards east of the Britannia, led to The Waverley Tavern, a celebrated 'museum' pub. It also led to the back entrance of The Institution, one of Glasgow's oldest taverns. Regulars would point out the iron ring, to which, according to oral tradition, Sir Walter Scott tethered his horse when he came to Glasgow to attend the Courthouse in Jail Square (and perhaps also to collect material for his novel *Rob Roy*). The old tavern's front entrance was in King Street.

O'Neill's

75 Albion Street, G1
0141 553 4040

Originally opened in 1998 as The Fruitmarket and Firkin, a real ale pub with in-house micro-brewery, this establishment became a branch of the O'Neill's 'Irish' pub chain in 2001. The open-planned interior has been remodelled and, with Victorian-style bar fittings and screens, is undeniably an improvement.

This section of the Merchant City is dominated by the City Hall and Markets, which had their origins in Albion Street Bazaar. It was divided into two sections: one accommodated the weekly market for dairy produce, while the other housed shops. The City Hall was built over the Bazaar in 1861. Among eminent Victorians who appeared in the City Hall was Charles Dickens, who later remarked that he had 'never been more heartily received anywhere or enjoyed myself so completely' as in Glasgow. In 1866, Glaswegians paid between 1/- and 4/- to hear Dickens read *A Christmas Carol* in the City Hall.

In 1885, the fruit market was extended along Candleriggs and Bell Street. The market moved to the northern outskirts of Glasgow in 1969, and the original Albion Street Bazaar became an atmospheric venue for jazz and folk festivals.

Oblomov

24 Candleriggs G1
0141 552 4251

Atmospheric 1990s café/bar/restaurant where the walls are lined with dark-stained tongued and grooved boards. This simple but effective 'matchboard' treatment was ubiquitous in the city's Victorian pubs and can still be seen to perfection in The Victoria Bar, Bridgegate. It went out of fashion in the 1890s when manufacturers introduced durable wall coverings such as lincrusta and anaglypta.

The **Old College Bar**

219 High Street, G1
0141 552 0940

Until the late 1980s, a small, attractive late-Victorian or Edwardian pub with an island bar and several handsome mirror advertisements. Now a friendly but nondescript lounge bar. The only mirror still *in situ* advertises George Younger and Sons' Alloa Ales. In the early 1900s, the proprietor of this pub made up his own blends of whisky - 'Old Coll' and 'Hooch Aye'.

The name of this traditional local recalls the old College or University of Glasgow, which stood opposite, for over four centuries. In 1679, the Principal and Masters of the College informed the Town Council that 'some persones keeps bulzard [billiard] tables, to the prejudice of the young men, their scholars, frequenting the same neir the Colledge, quhen they sould be att their books'.

By the 1860s, the University was surrounded by densely populated and disease-ridden slums. Young gentlemen scholars were also under moral siege. The area teemed with brothels. The University authorities sold their historic seat of learning to a railway company and moved west, to Gilmorehill.

The **Oriental Bar**

11 Hutcheson Street, G1
0141 552 3175

In the 1890s, this pub was a favourite with music hall artistes. The bar counter here was originally semi-circular. Mirrors, advertising Salt and Co.'s Burton Ales and Aitchison's Edinburgh Ales, graced the walls. Landlord John Baillie also sold the 'Oriental' blend of Scotch whiskies. The Oriental Bar is now a pseudo-Victorian lounge bar, handy for the Argyle Street shopping precinct. Live music Mon-Fri-Sat. Sunday night karaoke.

The leading Glasgow tavern of the 1830s – Jamie Begg's – was located in Hutcheson Street. The street, formed in 1791, crossed the grounds of 17th century Hutcheson's Hospital, which had its principal façade on Trongate, and gardens extending as far as Back Cow Loan (Ingram Street). The Hospital owed its existence to George and Thomas Hutcheson. Lawyer and landowner George Hutcheson was also a money lender with aristocrats among his clients.

Most of his wealth went to younger brother Thomas, along with instructions to establish an alms house for old men. Thomas committed over 20,000 'merks' of his own to lodge and educate 12 'indigent orphanes', laying the foundations of two famous grammar schools.

The **Polo Lounge**

84 Wilson Street, G1
0141 553 1221

Upmarket gay bar and nightclub with opulent *faux* decor – described as 'best in the world' by top UK gay newspaper, *Boyz*. Features gilt mirrors, chaise lounges and statues. Winner of Gaytime TV 'Gay Venue of the Year' award 1999. Open until 2am.

In the 1960s, there was a pub in Wilson Street called The Hangman's Rest, the walls of which were decorated with murals relating to the time when public executions took place outside the Tolbooth at Glasgow Cross. After performing his duty, the town's executioner fancied a swally. But, because of his odious occupation, he was unwelcome in the douce taverns of High Street and Trongate. According to legend, he was obliged to slink away to a tavern well away from the main drinking circuit.

Rab Ha's

83 Hutcheson Street, G1
0141 572 0400

Traditional bar/restaurant/ hotel, located in a late 18th-century warehouse. À la carte

menu served 5.30pm till late. Two-course pre-theatre set menu served 5.30-7.45 daily. This popular hostelry is named after Robert Hall, 'the Gleska glutton', a celebrated food junkie of early Victorian times.

Rat and Parrot

18 John Street, G1
0141 552 3801

Currently part of Scottish Brewers' Rat and Parrot chain, this used to be The Brewhouse and The John Street Jam. It's a cavernous pub on three levels built around a wood-panelled island bar, and was originally the John Street United Presbyterian Church. Regrettably, the alterations now hide a magnificent plaster ceiling. The central location makes The Rat and Parrot a favourite with office workers and students from the nearby University of Strathclyde. Breakfast is served here, and a full menu is also available.

The **Riggs**

11-13 Candleriggs, G1
0141 552 2126

There has been a tavern here since at least the 1840s. The present pub is a friendly well-run local with a sparse sub-*art moderne* decor. The Riggs was once a late-Victorian pub, however, and it still retains a magnificent mirror, advertising Steel, Coulson and Co's Stout and India Pale Ale; a rare example of the work of the Glasgow firm of H B McPhail and Co., whose products are now seldom seen *in situ*. In the early 1890s, the firm's showrooms were in London Street (now London Road), near Glasgow Cross. In the late 19th century, lavishly decorated mirrors were used widely for advertising purposes and

were distributed to pubs by brewers, distillers and spirit wholesalers. The example in The Riggs features a colourful view of Victorian Trongate.

The **Steps Bar**

62 Glassford Street, G1
0141 552 3059

A classic lounge bar of the 1930s. Its 'streamlined' Hollywood *art moderne* styling would have suited Raymond Chandler's private eye Philip Marlowe down to the ground. The stained glass window in the sitting-room depicts the Cunard liner *Queen Mary*, built at John Brown's Clydebank shipyard. Though the first keel plates were laid in 1930, the ship was not launched until 1934. The unfinished shell towered over Depression-stricken Clydebank for over two years.

The **Strathduie Bar**

3 Blackfriars Street, G1
0141 572 0934

In bygone days an Edwardian pub, this well-run local has escaped Merchant City gentrification and consists of a traditional 'men's shoap' bar and unisex lounge.

In the Middle Ages, the convent of the Dominicans, or Black Friars, stood on the east side of High Street, and

it was there that Edward I of England lodged, in 1301. At the Reformation, the University of Glasgow received the convent as a gift from the Crown. The Franciscans, or Grey Friars, also had a convent in this vicinity; it was situated on the south side of present George Street and entered from the west side of High Street by a lane which acquired the name Grey Friars Wynd. With the arrival of the railway, Blackfriars Street was relocated west of the High Street.

Tron Theatre
Café-bar

63 Trongate, G1
0141 552 8587

The Tron Theatre's popular Chisholm Street café-bar was redesigned in the late 1990s and now offers a bright and cheerful glass-walled ambience. A light menu is available in the café-bar until 10pm, with more substantial à la carte fare in the adjoining dark-panelled neo-Victorian restaurant, housed in a former church hall, and boasting a traditional long bar, set off by an elegant gantry. Good value pre-theatre menu served 5-7pm. Sunday brunch available from 10.30am to 4pm. Happy hours: Mon-Sat 5-7pm.

The Tron Kirk, originally the pre-Reformation collegiate church of St Mary and St Anne, was set ablaze in February 1793 by drunken members of the Hellfire Club, but the free-standing tower survived. The church was rebuilt in simplified style by James Adam, leaving the old tower free-standing,

as before. A 'trone', used to weigh market produce, was located outside this tower.

The **Waxworks**

20 Candleriggs, G1
0141 552 8717

Formerly known as Paddy O'Brian's Dream and Waxy's, and recently refurbished, this is now an unpretentious pub with a varied clientele. Inexpensive menu available daily from noon until 4pm. Happy hours 5-7pm. DJs Fri. Live local bands Sat.

Candleriggs was originally a pathway through cornfields, which were let out in 'riggs', or strips. After the great fire of 1652, Glasgow's candle makers were exiled to the edge of the riggs, as a safety measure. Despite this precaution, a second fire broke out in 1677 and destroyed 130 houses and shops.

In Victorian times, Glasgow's 'wax museum' was located in nearby Trongate. It had several incarnations under various owners and ended up as part of A E Pickard's leisure empire.

EAST END

Until the 1950s a hive of industry, Glasgow's east end extends out from Glasgow Cross by way of Gallowgate, Duke Street and London Road. The area, originally centred on the textile centre of Bridgeton, was a traditional working class part of the city, and most of the old closely packed tenements, thrown up to house the 19th-century labour force, were swept away during comprehensive development. After Gorbals, the east end bore the brunt of post-war planning mistakes – though it has so far escaped the proposed east flank of the Inner Ring Road. In 1951 145,000 people lived in the area. By the mid-1970s there were only 45,000.

In former times, there were many handsome pubs in the east end. And, since much of the area was built up in the early 1900s, many of the pubs were representative of the avant-garde 'Glasgow Style'. By 1939 there were also many art deco pubs in this area of heavy industry, which, after suffering greatly during the Depression of the early 1930s, experienced a mini-boom due to rearmament in the run-up to Hitler's war. Nowadays there are any number of nondescript pubs throughout the district. With a few exceptions (such as The Barrachnie Inn and The Portland Arms) those of interest generally lie close to Glasgow Cross.

The **Alexandra Bar**

468-470 Duke Street, G31
0141 556 2209

Named after Queen Alexandra, Consort of King Edward the Seventh, during whose reign (1902-10) much of Glasgow's east end was rebuilt on an impressive scale. Originally, this pub would have had a 'Glasgow Style' interior. Now it's a pastiche Edwardian pub with an island bar, and walls that are adorned with references to old Glasgow. Good traditional local, with beers and spirits served at rock-bottom prices (even cheaper on Sundays).

Duke Street is the UK's longest street, several yards longer than London's Regent Street. It opened in 1794, as Carntyne Road. It was renamed, supposedly after the Duke of Montrose.

The **Barrachnie Inn**

192 Glasgow Road, G32
0141 771 1607

In the early 20th century, thanks to Glasgow's splendid tramway system, outlying suburbs became increasingly attractive to day-trippers. Spirit merchant Gilbert Stewart commissioned Glasgow architects MacWhannel and Rogerson to create a splendid new pub, which he called Gilbert Stewart's Vaults. The firm had already designed one of the finest 'Glasgow Style' pubs in the city, The St Mungo Vintners in Queen Street, but the inn at Barrachnie was probably their finest achievement in pub design.

The new hostelry, opened in 1906, was situated in a picturesque, detached, Arts and Crafts-style building. The interior was similar to that of The St Mungo Vintners, with a long, art nouveau, mahogany bar, curved at the ends.

Nothing remains of MacWhannel and Rogerson's original sophisticated decor. The present interior, comfortable but nondescript, cannot compensate for the loss of one representative of the brief period when Glasgow led the world in avant-garde design. Inexpensive bar snacks and meals.

The **Bowler's Rest**

57 Tollcross Road, G31
0141 554 7585

A friendly but nondescript lounge bar, housed in a single-storey building, a relic of old Parkhead village. Inexpensive pub grub. Live entertainment.

In the early 19th-century, a wynd known as Montgomerie's Opening led to the Parkhead bowling green and Montgomerie's Tavern, forerunner of the present Bowler's Rest. In 1853, a breakaway group from the bowling club formed the Belvidere Bowling Club with a green on Elba Lane – now occupied by Barr's aerated water factory. The BBB is still in existence.

Chrystal, Bell & Co

31 Gallowgate, G1
0141 552 2690

First owned by Rutherford & Co. in the 1870s, and acquired by Finlay Stuart

Bell, of Chrystal, Bell & Co., in 1904, this-long-established hostelry was taken over by Scottish Brewers in the 1960s. 'Chrystal Bell' was an amalgamation of two families: the Chrystals, who were spirit merchants and distillery owners, and the Bells, who were shipowners. The present U-shaped bar here occupies a fraction of the floor space of the original Edwardian island bar but the capitals of the pillars supporting structural beams are original and reminiscent of the style of Alexander 'Greek' Thomson. Bar meals served 12-5 daily.

The **Drum**

1071 Shettleston Road, G32
0141 573 3220

Friendly east end local with typical 1980s decor. Inexpensive bar lunches. Live entertainment.

The present pub occupies one half of a long-redundant billard hall, erected on the site of The Old Drum Tavern, one of the most famous howffs in the east end. In the 1890s The Old Drum was a single-storey building with a thatched roof. Legend has it that the district brass band practised in the tavern, the landlord playing the big drum.

The **Hielan Jessie**

374 Gallowgate, G40
0141 552 0753

A comparatively new pub, situated in one of two fine 1771 tenements. The bar has a low ceiling, a long bar and other traditional features. Interesting photographs by the late Oscar Marzaroli decorate the walls. Handy for the weekend Barras street market.

The original Highland Jessie Tavern stood at 328 Gallowgate. It was the haunt of soldiers from Gallowgate Barracks. 'Hielan Jessie' is supposed to have been Jessie Brown, a soldier's wife among besieged Europeans in Lucknow during the Sepoy mutiny of 1857. At a critical moment during the siege, Jessie allegedly heard the sound of Highland bagpipes above the din of battle. She

rallied the exhausted defenders, and soon they also heard the pipes of the relief force – the 78th Highlanders. According to press stories, Jessie was fêted by senior officers, who drank her health while pipers marched round the table playing Auld Lang Syne. She became a Victorian heroine, a fit subject for 'imperishable verse':

Ye heroes of Lucknow, fame
crowns you with glory,
Love welcomes you home
with glad songs in your
praise,
And brave Jessie Brown, with
her soul-stirring story,
For ever will live in the
Highlanders' lays.

The **Kirk House**

1365 Shettleston Road, G32
0141 778 1624

Mock-Victorian pub. The original inn on this site took its name from the adjacent 'Auld Kirk' of Shettleston. By the Edwardian period, the site of the old inn was occupied by a red sandstone tenement incorporating a pub called The Kirk House. It was remodelled in 1937, with a brick and faience 'streamlined' exterior. The interior was stylish art moderne, with an island bar.

The **Ladywell**

139 Barrack Street, G4
0141 552 2048

Formerly part of a typical east end tenement, this spartan but well-run lounge bar stands in isolation opposite Tennent's Wellpark Brewery.

The pub takes its name from the historic Lady Well behind the present brewery. The Well was dedicated to the Virgin Mary in medieval times. In the early 19th century it was used as a public drinking fountain. It fell into disuse after the Glasgow Necropolis, a magnificent cemetery on the lines of Paris's Père Lachaise, was opened nearby.

A major asset of John and Robert Tennent's Wellpark Brewery was an abundant supply of soft, pure water, drawn from a deep well within the brewery. Rival

brewers had to use the Molendinar burn – which eventually became a public sewer. In the 1830s, Tennent's porter was sold as far afield as Liverpool, from where it was shipped to North and South America. In the early 1890s, a complete lager beer brewery – the first in Scotland – was built at Wellpark and brewing commenced under the supervision of German brewer Jacob Klingler. Within a few years, Tennent's Pilsener lager beer had won a string of prestigious awards.

The **Old Black Bull**

1316 Gallowgate, G31
0141 551 0400

A long-established Parkhead local, now a comfortable lounge bar, which perpetuates the name of the district's most famous hostelry.

In the late 18th century, Parkhead was a weaving village. The centre of community life was The Black Bull Inn, founded 1760, and immortalised in verse by a local bard, John Breckinridge:

It's auld Ne'erday, an' we're
i' the 'Bull',
Wi' our hearts dancin' licht,
an' a bowl flowing full,
Let envy and spite throw aff
a' disguise,
And drink to young Gibbie
that's ge'en us the pies.

'Young Gibbie' was master baker Gilbert Watson, who was also the local postmaster, with a bakery cum post office at the corner of Westmuir Street and Great Eastern Road.

The **Old Burnt Barns**

183 London Road, G1

A friendly, popular local, handy for the Barras weekend market. Victorian-style interior with a traditional long bar and gantry. Large comfortable lounge.

In 1668, a range of malt barns in St Mungo's Loan was destroyed by fire. The original Burnt Barns Inn bore

the date 1679 and stood at the junction of South St Mungo Street and Great Hamilton Street, on or near the site of the blaze. It had a courtyard and stables and fronted Glasgow Green (London Road didn't exist at that time).

The **Portland Arms**

1169 Shettleston Road, G32
0141 778 6657

In the late 1930s, the rise of Nazi Germany led to rearmament – and salvation for Glasgow's hard-pressed heavy industries. After years of unemployment, workers had money in their pockets. Some of it was spent in handsome new pubs, such as The Portland Arms. In 1938, landlord Jonathan Tyndal built the present pub beside the old Portland Arms – a low-ceilinged vernacular hostelry. The new pub was in 'streamlined' art moderne style. By 1939, thanks to the mini-boom of the period, there were many similar pubs in the east end.

The B listed Portland Arms was contemporary with the Empire Exhibition, held in Glasgow's Bellahouston Park between May and October, 1938. There's a classic *art moderne* lighting canopy (currently disused) above a splendid island bar, banded with exotic veneers. The pub may have lost its original geometric-patterned floorcovering, but otherwise, it's extremely well-preserved,

with a range of original sitting rooms (by 1938 women were being welcomed into new lounge bars such as The Portland Arms).

A great evocation of the stylish 1930s, in an area where the standard of pub design is now very poor.

The **Railway Tavern**

1416 Shettleston Road, G32
0141 778 2368

This friendly little pub of character occupies an old single-storey building. The original art nouveau etched windows have vanished, but the Edwardian interior survives with a low-ceilinged bar, island counter, central gantry and snugs.

In the 18th century, Shettleston – sometimes spelt 'Shuttleston' – was a weaving village. In 1242, King Alexander II granted the lands of Schedinestun to the Bishop of Glasgow and his successors. The arrival of the North British Railway (1871) encouraged industry. Between 1890 and 1900, the parish doubled in population.

The **Tavern**

194 Tollcross Road, G31
0141 554 8498

This popular local, east of Parkhead Cross, dates from 1930 and is a fine example of the mock-Tudor fashion of the period. South of the Tweed, huge roadhouses in this nostalgic idiom sprang up along new arterial highways. The exterior has lost original

interesting textures – timber appliqué, roughcast, and brick in herring-bone patterns – but the interior is well-preserved, with a low beamed ceiling and art deco bar.

In the 13th century, King Alexander III prohibited the bailies and sergeants of the Royal Burgh of Rutherglen from collecting tolls in Glasgow. Rutherglen was allowed to collect them at the cross of Shettleston – hence the name Tollcross.

The **Saracen Head** Bar

209 Gallowgate, G1
0141 552 1660

Opened in 1905 and long known as the 'Sarry Heid', this pub, handy for Glasgow's famous Barras market, is prominent in the city's folklore. The frontage has painted panels depicting the old College (High Street) and the original Saracen's Head Inn. A traditional long bar and gantry are features here, along with a collection of bric-a-brac. For many years this pub has specialised in cider, which used to be sold from small barrels of over four gallons capacity.

Extravagant historical claims have been made for the 'Sarry Heid', but it's not particularly old – even by Glasgow standards. The name recalls The Saracen's Head Inn, used by James Boswell and Samuel Johnson on their return from their tour of the Highlands and Hebrides (1773). Built by Robert Tennent – co-founder of Wellpark Brewery – in 1755, it stood at the foot of Great Dovehill. The new inn was built on the burial ground of Little St Mungo's Chapel. Victorian historian Robert Reid, who wrote under the pen-name 'Senex' observed: 'It was certainly rather a queer idea to plant an inn in a kirkyard, converting the graves into wine cellars and kitchens as was actually the case.'

In July 1778, when the first London-Glasgow mail coach arrived at The Saracen's Head, passengers were greeted by black waiters in embroidered coats, red plush breeches, and powdered wigs. The 405-mile journey had taken 66 hours.

That same year, when the city fathers raised the Glasgow Royal Volunteers, 'to enable His Majesty to quell the present unnatural rebellion in America', recruiting officers paraded with colours flying and

drums beating, then adjourned to The Saracen's Head Inn, where they distributed free drink to the populace gathered round a huge bonfire in Gallowgate.

The inn was sold in 1792 and converted into shops and flats but some original features were left untouched. In the 1890s, the ballroom was used as a mission hall and Sunday school. The inn's blue and white china punch bowl, decorated with Glasgow's coat of arms and the motto 'Success to the town of Glasgow', is preserved in the People's Palace museum.

In the early 19th century, an inn called The New Saracen's Head was built on the opposite side of Gallowgate. William and Dorothy Wordsworth used it when they visited Glasgow.

The **Seven Ways**

621 London Road, G40
0141 551 9543

The name of this popular local, a refurbished 1950s lounge bar, refers to the seven roads and streets which converged on Bridgeton Cross, after the area was redeveloped around the hub of the present ornate cast-iron pavilion (1874), built by the Sun Foundry, and popularly called the 'Brigton Umbrella'.

Nowadays the standard of east end pubs leaves much to be desired, and it's difficult to credit that a century ago, there were many palatial pubs in the district. In 1893, Hillcoat's Bar at Bridgeton Cross boasted a huge mirror, alleged to be the largest in any pub in Glasgow. The cellars accommodated 50 hogsheads of Younger's and McEwan's beers. In the early 1900s, one of the finest pubs in the area was The Shawfield Bar in Main Street. The ornate fittings were of walnut, maple, oak and mahogany, and the new-fangled electroliers were of oxydised silver.

Bridgeton, originally Bridge Town, takes its name from an early 18th century timber bridge which linked Glasgow with Rutherglen. In the 1830s, Bridgeton had over 2,000 hand-loom weavers and was a centre of artisan radicalism.

If time permits, walk the short distance west along London Road to the old Calton graveyard in Abercromby Street. In 1787, a group of weavers, rioting in protest against severe reductions in wage rates, were fired on by the military. Three were killed outright, and another three were mortally wounded. Over 6,000 sympathisers attended the dead weavers' funeral in the Calton burying-ground. Glasgow's magistrates rewarded the soldiers with gifts of stockings and shoes.

The character of Glasgow changes dramatically once the Clyde has been crossed. Until the comprehensive development years of the 1960s and 70s, no such change would have been discerned – for Victorian and Edwardian Gorbals had the same urban distinction as the rest of the city, with well-built Victorian tenements flanking bustling streets. Today's Gorbals has less than a quarter of its 1950s population, though tenements of traditional design are rising again in the area. At one time Gorbals had the largest concentration of pubs on the south side – and as late as 1948, there were 174 pubs in the district.

The south side beyond Gorbals is a huge area covering old towns and villages long absorbed into the city proper – such as Govan, Strathbungo and Cathcart. Since districts such as Pollokshields were among the most prosperous in the late-Victorian city, the south side also boasts some stunning architecture. But middle class Glasgow suburbs of the 19th century were practically devoid of pubs and are comparatively 'pub free' to the present day. Consequently, most of the interesting south side pubs are within easy reach of the city centre.

The Allison Arms

720 Pollokshaws Road, G41
0141 423 1661

A traditional unpretentious local with an exterior of roughcast and crazily patterned artificial stone. It's somewhat spartan internally, but the original U-shaped bar survives along with a carved gantry graced with a handsome etched mirror advertising William Younger's ales. This pioneering real ale pub still sells fine cask-conditioned beers, along with a large selection of single malt whiskies (Malt of the Month at a bargain price). Happy hours 11am-5pm Mon-Sat. Live entertainment every Sat.

Alphabet Yard

15 Millbrae Road, G41
0141 649 6861

Attractive minimalist bar/restaurant, housed in a cubist art deco building (1937-9), formerly a Corporation Lighting Department designed by Sam Bunton, who was also responsible for some stylish art deco pubs in the Glasgow of the 1930s. Bunton went on to design the notorious Red Road tower blocks, the tallest such buildings in Scotland.

The split-level bar interior is relaxed and pleasant, with genuflections in the direction of stylish 1930s *art moderne.* Bar food served from midday till 5pm daily. Children's menu available till 8 pm daily in the restaurant.

The **Bay Horse**

964 Pollokshaws Road, G41

In 1899, a licensed trade journal described this pub as 'a commodious and elegantly-appointed establishment'. It was remodelled in the 1930s and, until the early 1990s, retained a classic *art moderne* exterior, with neon-lit fascia lettering. Sadly, it's now a nondescript mock-Victorian bar. Happy hours Sat-Sun, opening time till 9pm.

The **Boswell Hotel**

27 Mansionhouse Road, G41
0141 632 9812

In the 1980s, this converted Victorian mansion house, situated in the hilly suburb of Langside, was a real ale mecca, offering a rotating selection of Scottish and English brews, augmented by an extraordinary array of continental bottled beers. There are still well-kept ales to be had here, but stocks of European bottled beers are now limited. Good value bar snacks and meals are available throughout the day until mid-evening, and the adjoining beer garden is a popular summer feature. Children welcome.

The **Brazen Head**

1 Cathcart Road, G42
0141 420 1530

Formerly The Granite City Bar, and one of the few old pubs to survive the comprehensive development of Gorbals. There are traces of art nouveau, but the pub's now a busy Irish bar, situated in a Victorian building fronting a disused railway viaduct. Refurbished in the 1990s, the bar was extended through one of the viaduct arches. Live Irish music.

In the 1780s, a Mrs Balmanno kept an apothecary shop in the Trongate, trading 'at the sign of the Brazen Head'. Her shop sign was a 'brazen' (brass) effigy of the Ancient Greek physician Galen.

Brechin's Bar

803 Govan Road, G51
0141 445 1349

Situated in the mock-baronial Cardell Halls, built in 1894 by John Cardell – an implacable enemy of 'Demon Drink' – as a centre for temperance workers, this was originally a grand Edwardian pub, built for William Brechin and Sons. It's now a popular bar/lounge with a 1950s-style island bar. Inexpensive bar lunches.

According to legend, the carving of a cat on the building's Burleigh Street façade commemorates felines who eliminated a plague of rats brought to the town by ships bringing flax to the weavers of Govan. Until the removal of industrial grime, the neighbouring statue of shipbuilder Sir William Pearce was known as the 'Black Man'.

In the late 16th century, when the chief industries were salmon-fishing and farming, Govan was described as 'a gret and ane large village upon the watir of clyde ... it brewis gude ale commended through the hail land'. In May 1651, Tammas Smythe of Teucharhill, Govan, was appointed by the minister and elders to come to Govan Kirk on Sunday and 'declair his sorrow for being ane drunken man in presence of ye congregationne, and be rebukit'.

In the late 18th century, on New Year's Day, Glasgow's hoi polloi converged on Govan for the 'sport' of cock-shooting. The cock was tied to a stake, and the price of a shot was one penny. Whoever killed the bird took it home for dinner. As late as the 1820s, Govan was still a place of thatched cottages set in zigzagging wynds and lanes. Glasgow folk made Sunday excursions to the village for salmon suppers. By 1839, weaving was the staple industry. Govan weavers took their ease in The Sheephead Inn, which had a fine garden. Among other old howffs were The Stag Inn, The Thistle Inn, and The Black Bull Tavern. Shipbuilding was introduced in 1841, and by the time the burgh was annexed by Glasgow, in 1912, the population had grown to 90,000.

The **Church On The Hill**

16 Algie Street, G41
0141 649 5189

A bar/restaurant located in the former Langside Free Church, designed by a pupil of Alexander Thomson. Money ran out before the pediment sculpture – John

Knox, Mary Queen of Scots and Regent Moray – could be carried out. In the 1980s this grandiose classical pile was a burnt-out shell. A large island bar serves both bar and restaurant areas, and there's

some interesting if idiosyncratic modern stained glass. Large and varied fare includes pre-theatre menu, served 5pm-7pm. DJs Fri-Sun. Happy hours noon-7pm. In good weather, you can drink and dine al fresco.

The nearby monument was erected in 1887 to commemorate the Battle of Langside, the decisive engagement of the Wars of Reformation. In May 1568, Queen Mary's army was routed by Regent Moray's smaller army, fighting from the vantage point of Langside Hill. Six hundred Glasgow men fought on Moray's side.

The **Clockwork Beer Company**

1153/55 Cathcart Road, G42
0141 649 0184

Opened in 1997, this micro-brewery and bar/restaurant is owned and run by Robin and Gay Graham, formerly of the Boswell Hotel, Mansionhouse Road (see entry). The Grahams turned The Boswell into a real ale oasis, to which enthusiasts journeyed from near and far. Aficionados now flock to the art deco-fronted Clockwork Brewery, which is located in the premises of a former wholesale clothier. The micro-brewery can be viewed through plate glass and its products consumed in attractive surroundings, with a mezzanine level, a no smoking section and a children's area, replete with games and toys.

The micro-brewery is a small five-barrel facility, which means it can make up to 1440 pints at a time. The beers are dispensed from antique Aitken tall fonts. In addition to home-brewed ales, wheat beers, fruit beers, stouts, and lager beers, this admirable hostelry also offers a wide range of Belgian and German bottled beers, a fine selection of malt whiskies, and a huge variety of non-alcoholic beverages. The wine list features traditional Scottish fruit wines, including Cairn O'Mohr bramble, elderberry, raspberry, and strawberry wines, produced in Errol, a village in the Carse of Gowrie. The adventurous can also sample cowslip, gooseberry, rhubarb, damson, and bilberry. In earlier centuries, the 'guidwife' knew how to make wines and cordials from flowers, berries, vegetables, grains and even tree sap – notably birch and spruce. Food is served from opening time, with last orders taken Mon-Thur 8.45pm; Fri, Sat and Sun 9.45pm. Children's hours – opening time till 8pm. Live traditional music on Tuesday nights. Live jazz on Tuesday nights. Blues on Sunday nights.

The **Corona**

1039 Pollokshaws Road, G41
0141 632 6230

Built in 1912-13 by Clarke and Bell for spirit merchant James O'Mally, The Corona survived in pristine condition until the late 1990s, when its

unspoilt interior was drastically remodelled. The pub, now part of the John Barras chain, retains a distinctive exterior, with a diminutive turret crowned by a cupola. The basic interior structure, featuring a conservatory-style glazed roof, carried on cast-iron columns and elliptical arches, remains, but the new open-planned bar is a poor substitute for the original bar and snugs which, though built on the eve of WW1, had strong affinities with the famous 'Glasgow Style'. The usual amenities of city pub chains are on offer here, including good value bar lunches. Disco every Friday and Saturday.

Above The Corona's entrances are sculptural representations of a right hand, palm outward, with a superimposed Passion-Cross. These allude to the curiously named village of Crossmyloof which formerly occupied the Shawlands Cross area. 'Cross my loof' is old Scots dialect for 'cross my palm'. According to folklore, Mary Queen of Scots passed through the district shortly before the Battle of Langside, displayed an ebony cross in the palm of her hand, and declared that 'by the cross in my loof' she would defeat the Regent Moray's army in battle. It has been suggested that the name Crossmyloof comes from the Gaelic Crois Moaldhuibh, the cross of Malduff, an early Celtic saint.

Finlay's

137 Kilmarnock Road, G41
0141 636 4444

A comfortable low-ceilinged, split-level lounge bar. Basic pub menu, served from midday until 5pm weekdays, Sat 12-4. DJs on Saturdays.

The Fotheringay

21 Nithsdale Road, G41
0141 424 5051

A popular and well-run local, consisting of a lounge, snug

bar and cellar bar/restaurant. Reasonably-priced pub food, served from 12 noon until 8.30pm (12 noon until 9.45 Thu-Sat). DJs Fridays and Saturdays.

The South Side of Glasgow, scene of the Battle of Langside, abounds in romantic references to Mary Queen of Scots. It was in Fotheringay Castle that she was beheaded, on 18 February, 1587.

The **Gairdener's Arms**

272 Paisley Road, G5
0141 420 1272

This large informal split-level pub opened in time for the 1998 Glasgow Garden Festival. Beer garden. Bar meals served from midday until early evening.

Nearby, with a motorway flyover as its neighbour, is one of Glasgow's most magnificent Victorian warehouses, built for the Scottish Co-operative Wholesale Society in 1892-97. Architects Bruce and Hay recycled the French Second Empire-style design from their City Chambers competition entry of 1880! Atop the dome, the personification of 'Light and Liberty' is a Glasgow landmark.

The **Georgic Bar**

1097 Pollokshaws Road, G41
0141 632 2317

Popular and long-established local. The public bar retains authentic 1930s fittings. The Georgic is still a traditional 'men's shoap' – more or less. But in 1996, as a concession to the Zeitgeist, a small mock-Victorian lounge bar (with ladies' toilet) was added to the premises. Inexpensive lunch menu. Live entertainment every Sunday afternoon.

The **Granary**

10 Kilmarnock Road, G41
0141 632 8487

A superior bar/diner, dating from 1983, with a main bar and separate rooms for eating and drinking. In the bar, the counter boasts an impressive canopy embellished with carved wooden effigies of winged females. Food includes pre-theatre menu, served Fri-Sat-Sun 5.30pm-7pm. Breakfast served on Sundays. This prominent site, at the junction of Pollokshaws Road and Kilmarnock Road, was formerly occupied by a famous Samuel Dow pub.

Heraghty's Free House

708 Pollokshaws Road, G41
0141 423 0380

In Scotland a 'free house' is a pub which is not financially tied to a brewery. It does not

mean that customers can enjoy lavish hospitality at the expense of the owner. A long-established no-frills pub with strong Irish associations, Heraghty's is basically Edwardian, featuring an elegant carved gantry, adorned with mirrors. In the 1930s, in a fit of extravagance, there was added an art deco transom light, in stained glass. When the first edition of *The Glasgow Pub Companion* was published, in 1996, this howff did not boast a ladies' loo. The pub has since been equipped with that useful amenity. Heraghty's caters largely for a dedicated south side clientele and even sponsors a local football team – Heraghty's Heroes.

The **Honours Three**

231 St Andrew's Road, G41
0141 423 0380

A large, comfortable, mock-Tudor bar and lounge. Good value meals served Mon-Sat 12-3. Karaoke evenings and 60s and 70s discos.

The name refers to the Regalia, anciently styled 'The Honours of Scotland', embracing the Crown, Sceptre and Sword of State – among the oldest crown jewels in Europe. Between September 1651 and May 1652, the 'Honours' were hidden in Dunnottar Castle, in Kincardineshire. They were smuggled out of the castle and taken to the Reverend James Grainger, minister of the neighbouring parish of Kinneff. Grainger hid them in his kirk until the Restoration. The 'Honours' were displayed at the Scots Parliament until 1707, after which they lay undisturbed in an oak chest in Edinburgh Castle. Through the persistent lobbying of arch romantic Sir Walter Scott, the relics were restored to public display in 1818.

The **Jeanie**

6 Dinmont Road, G41
0141 632 3615

Near Shawland Cross, this is a modern free-standing pub

on two levels, consisting of a well-appointed lounge bar/restaurant and public bar (upstairs). Good value meals and snacks. Live music in the public bar Thu nights and karaoke at weekends. Car park and beer garden. The Jeanie takes its name from Jeanie Deans, heroine of Walter Scott's novel *The Heart of Midlothian* (1818).

The **Mission**

160 Battlefield Road, G41
0141 649 7818

Large, split-level lounge bar/diner with low ceilings and back-lit stained glass. Frequented by students and staff from the nearby Victoria Infirmary. Basic bar menu. Regular DJs. Happy hours: 11am-7pm daily.

1901

1534 Pollokshaws Road, G43
0141 632 0161

Located in a conspicious *fin-de-siècle* 'Glasgow Style' corner tenement. The original pub was contemporary with the building (1901) – but the art nouveau interior has vanished. The present pub/restaurant is well-run and friendly. It's also a south side real ale oasis, with six regular and guest brews on offer. Live bands (folk, rock and jazz) Sat.

Until 1996 this hostelry was known as The Old Swan Inn. In the early 20th century, Glasgow's tramways were extended to peripheral towns and villages. Tenements rose on the sites of the old country inns with their cosy bar-parlours and adjoining gardens or bowling greens. The names of vanished hostelries were often perpetuated by the handsome Edwardian pubs that were features of the new tenements. These new pubs sometimes commemorated their predecessors by means of pictorial stained glass.

The Old Swan tenement has a secure niche in the history of conservation in Glasgow.

Its restoration in the early 1970s marked a change of policy emphasis, from draconian comprehensive development to rehabilitation of sound tenement stocks.

In 1677, several Pollokshavians were accused of 'bewitching' Sir George Maxwell of Pollok. Perhaps it was this incident that gave rise to the well-known saying 'the queer folk o' the Shaws'. By the mid-19th century, the former handloom weavers' village was a thriving little town. As late as 1891, there were 43 pubs in Pollokshaws, serving a population of around 10,000.

Napoleon's

128 Merrylee Road, G41
0141 629 1901

Cathcart was one of several Glasgow districts where the locals took advantage of the Temperance (Scotland) Act of 1913 and voted, in 1920, to become completely 'dry' (the others were Whiteinch, Pollokshields and Camphill). Consequently there are no old pubs in the district. Napoleon's is a modern, large, well-upholstered mock-Victorian lounge bar/diner. The split-level interior has lots of pictorial references to the Napoleonic wars and several portraits of Bonaparte in full Imperial rig. Good value bar fare available midday till late.

Nickie Tam's

510 Victoria Road, G41
0141 433 2431

Formerly The Old Vic, this hostelry re-opened in 1996 as a themed 'West Coast bothy' pub. Food, including traditional Scottish fare,

served 12-5 daily. Bargain beers Sun-Thur 7pm-11pm. DJs Fridays. Karaoke Saturdays.

The **Old Smiddy**

131 Old Castle Road, G44
0141 637 3284

A pleasant well-run Cathcart local in a historic village smithy, featuring a low-ceilinged, split-level interior embellished with agricultural bric-a-brac. Food served all day, seven days a week.

At one time Cathcart blacksmith Robert Peddie also did duty as the local vet. An outside stair led from the smithy to the Dogs' Infirmary. The smith's thatched cottage stood nearby until 1892, when a tenement was built on the site. Castle Road, renamed Old Castle Road in the 1920s, led to Cathcart Castle, a picturesque ruin demolished as recently as 1980. Cathcart, absorbed by Glasgow in 1912, was formerly a weaving village. In the 19th century, city dwellers turned it into a summer resort. For centuries, the village howff was known as The Wee Thack Hoose in the Glen. A two-storey whitewashed thatched house, it stood in Snuffmill Road, near the Old Cathcart Bridge. Summer tourists consumed strawberries and cream in the adjoining garden. For some forty years the licence was held by a local character, Grannie Robertson. When this historic tavern was demolished, in 1893, a two-handed sword was found in the roof thatch.

In 1920 the voters of Cathcart went 'dry', closing the district's four pubs. When saner times returned, The Old Smiddy was the first Cathcart hostelry to obtain a liquor licence.

The **Old Toll Bar**

1 Paisley Road West, G51
0141 429 3135

Consisting of a B listed Victorian bar and a modern basement lounge bar, this is one of Glasgow's hidden

treasures. The name perpetuates the memory of the Parkhouse Toll, which operated turnpike roads between Glasgow and Greenock, via Govan, and between Glasgow and Paisley, via the village of Halfwayhouse. The original proprietor of The Old Toll Bar was David McCall, a prominent Glasgow restaurateur. His customers enjoyed some choice liquors, including Smith's Glenlivet malt whisky and Robert Younger's famed 90/- Ale. As indicated on one of the mirrors, 'very old vintage port, brandy, champagnes and clarets' were provided for more fastidious patrons.

The pub exterior is mock-Victorian – the original frontage was discarded a long time ago. The inner doors are original, and contain delightful examples of Victorian painted glass. The unspoilt interior, dating from 1892, has a long bar and a magnificent gantry incorporating spirit casks. There were originally two tiers of barrels, but smaller casks were removed many years ago. Above dark polished wood panelling, the walls are covered with lincrusta-type material. The four superb advertisement mirrors, enriched with colours and gilding, were made by the Glasgow firm of Forrest and Son.

One mirror bears the

inscription 'pressure filtered Black and Gold, the aristocrat of whiskies' – a reminder that before it became compulsory to mature spirits in bond for a minimum period before retailing them, whisky was sometimes artificially 'aged', making it more palatable and less toxic.

The Old Toll Bar, now unique, was a typical Glasgow 'palace pub' of the 1890s. There were once dozens of similar pubs on the South Side – and hundreds more around the city.

The **Queen's Park Café**

530 Victoria Road, G42

Opened in 1899, near Queen's Park, which was laid out by Sir Joseph Paxton of Crystal Palace fame; the name commemorates Mary Queen of Scots, whose army was defeated at the Battle of Langside in 1568. Formerly a 'Glasgow Style' pub with sophisticated art nouveau interior, The Queen's Park Café is now mock-Victorian, with an island bar and nostalgic prints. This popular pub was the local of the late Mark McManus, star of Scottish Television's highly successful *Taggart* detective series.

In the late 1890s, the temperance movement was at the peak of its influence. The word 'pub' was anathema to the 'unco guid', and bar owners whose premises were situated in exclusive residential areas or smart city streets began to call their pubs 'cafés'.

In 1870, 'singing classes under Signor Cunio' were on the curriculum at the Carlton Institution for the Board and Education of Young Ladies, Dixon Avenue, Queen's Park. In 1894, Miss Mary Brown took off in a hot air balloon from the Grand National Carnival, Cathkin Park. Attired in a loose blouse and voluminous bloomers, she made a parachute descent from the balloon, landing safely in Queen's Park.

Samuel Dow's

69-71 Nithsdale Road, G41
0141 423 0107

Formerly a stylish 1930s *art moderne* lounge bar, now a popular south-side local, consisting of a busy main bar and a cosy first floor lounge. Live bands Fri-Sat. Good value lunch menu.

'Samuel Dow' was a famous name in Glasgow's drink trade. There had been a Samuel Dow in the Glasgow trade since at least 1807, and the tradition carried on through three generations, until 1895. In that year the last Samuel Dow died – as a boy he'd migrated from Lochaber to Glasgow in order to enter the wine and spirit establishment of his uncle; in due course he became one of the partners, and in 1881 sole partner. He was associated with the top end of the trade; in the 1880s he supplied city bar and restaurant owners with a range of champagnes, including Moët et Chandon, Veuve Clicquot and Perrier Jouets. 'Samuel Dow's Special Blend' of 'Old Highland Whisky' was exported to Australia, India, China, the USA and the Continent.

In the 17th century, the village of Strathbungo was inhabited by weavers and miners. Turn left on leaving Samuel Dow's and walk a few yards to 1-10 Moray Place, one of Alexander Thomson's

finest architecture compositions. In 1859, when Thomson designed this noble terrace, Strathbungo was on the southern outskirts of Glasgow. From 1860, the great architect lived at 1 Moray Place – the pedimented pavilion at the north end of the terrace. He died there in 1875.

Sharkey's

51 Old Rutherglen Road, G5
0141 429 3944

After draconian redevelopment, apparently by planners who were teetotal as well as blind, there are few pubs of any description in

Gorbals, which had some of the finest 'palace pubs' of the Victorian era. This modern pub is a basic bar and lounge, built into old railway arches behind the Citizens' Theatre. Live music sessions (traditional Scottish and Irish folk) in the lounge bar Mon and Sat. Inexpensive lunch menu available Mon-Sat.

In the Middle Ages, Glasgow's lepers were accommodated in St Ninian's Hospital, which stood on the Gorbals side of the river. Twice a week, they were allowed to enter the town to beg, always with a wooden clapper to warn people of their approach. Gorbals remained an insignificant suburb until the early 19th century, when cotton mills were built there. In 1826, the great Prussian architect Karl Friedrich Schinkel visited Todd's mill in Hutchesontown and was impressed by the 'enormous production ... all done by young girls, some of them very pretty'.

Under the City Improvement Act of 1866, old Gorbals village was swept away. In its turn, Victorian Gorbals was levelled to the ground in the comprehensive development years (1957-74). After disastrous experiments with tower blocks and deck-access flats, handsome new tenements of traditional design are currently rising in Gorbals.

Sir John Stirling Maxwell

Shawlands Arcade, G41
0141 636 9024

Useful café-bar located on the walkway of an unlovely 1960s shopping precinct overlooking Kilmarnock Road. The ambience is typical J D Wetherspoon, with pseudo-Victorian decor and a no-smoking area. Well-kept real ales. Full menu served 11am-10pm.

In 1805, a fiver was offered for information leading to the capture of Andrew Thomson, poacher, accused of shooting

partridges on Sir John Maxwell's estate at Newlands. 'Thomson is little more than twenty years of age, rather tall and of a fair complexion, wore a fustian jacket and corduroy breeches; had a game bag under his jacket, carried a double barrelled gun, and hunted with a large, brown and white pointer, very lean.'

The **Sou' Wester**

24 Bridge Street, G5
0141 429 2544

A 'sou' wester' is a strong wind from the southwest. But this popular local probably owes its name to its location at the southwest corner of Eglinton Street. When the first edition of *The Glasgow Pub Companion* appeared, this was a *fin-de-siècle* pub of character and a fascinating link with old Gorbals. It was completely unspoilt, with a semi-circular bar, screens and snugs. Glasgow's reign as 'City of Architecture and Design 1999' did nothing to save historic pubs – on the contrary, some of the city's last pubs of character disappeared in the late 1990s. In the present Sou' Wester, revamped in nondescript

open-planned fashion, there survives a relic of the original howff – a superb mirror, advertising David Nicholson's Palace Brewery, taken over by Edinburgh United Breweries in 1889.

Bridge Street, leading to Jamaica Bridge, divided Tradeston from Laurieston – pleasant new suburbs in the early 19th century. Before the major Victorian railway termini were built in Hope Street and St Enoch Square, the tiny railway station in Bridge Street handled 1.25 million passengers every year.

The **Taverna**

778 Pollokshaws Road, G41
0141 424 0858

This attractive establishment started life in the early 1990s as The Athena Taverna, a Greek-Cypriot bar/diner. Good

value business lunch available Mon-Fri 12-3. In addition to cask ales, there's a varied selection of bottled beers from Europe and the US.

The **Titwood Bar**

52 Nithsdale Road, G41
0141 423 0673

A friendly South Side local, situated in a a douce Thomsonesque terraced tenement. Tasty inexpensive bar meals served Mon-Fri 12-2.15, Sat 12-4.45.

The **Victoria Bar**

400 Victoria Road, G42
0141 423 4352

A friendly and well-patronised local which retains a superb *fin-de-siècle* frontage and 'Glasgow Style' etched glass. However, the original interior has been destroyed and the pub remodelled as a bar/lounge/diner. Inexpensive meals are served daily from midday until 2.30pm.

The **Village**

61 Kilmarnock Road, G41
0141 649 2745

A typical 1990s café-bar with a conservative neo-Victorian split-level interior. Inexpensive and varied bar food.

NORTH SIDE

By 1900 north Glasgow was a densely populated and predominantly working-class area. Springburn was home to the giant North British Locomotive Company, while the great Saracen Foundry dominated Possilpark. The area was a forest of factory chimneys, one of the tallest being 'Tennant's Stalk' at the St Rollox chemical works (450 feet). By 1950, before comprehensive development and urban motorways ripped the heart out of north Glasgow, Maryhill, Springburn and Possilpark were vibrant communities where the architectural module – as elsewhere in urban Glasgow – was the four-storey tenement block. Maryhill retains some original Victorian character, but Springburn and Possilpark have not recovered from the draconian experiments of town planners and motorway engineers. North of the Royal Infirmary, the once-populous district of Townhead has been transformed into the Townhead interchange, a soulless highway junction designed to serve as the nerve centre of a vast ring road system, most of which (thankfully) was never built. At one time north Glasgow had many famous taverns and inns. The HLI Bar, formerly at the corner of Maryhill Road and Kelvinside Avenue, had as its sign a kilted HLI soldier standing guard in a sentry box. Behind the bar there was a long mirror decorated with etched representations of soldiers in various uniforms of the regiment. Ye Olde Tramcar Vaults, corner of New City Road and Hopehill Road, had a model Edwardian single decker tramcar as its pub sign. Pubs of character are now few and far between in north Glasgow. Most of the nine pubs listed here are to be found in Maryhill.

The **Elephant and Bugle**

1397 Maryhill Road, G20
0141 946 2341

Lively and popular Maryhill local with an upstairs lounge bar. Inexpensive bar meals. Karaoke evenings.

Situated close to Wyndford housing estate (built on the site of Maryhill Barracks), this pub takes its name from the cap badge of the Highland Light Infantry, which became the official City of Glasgow regiment in 1923, and amalgamated with the Royal Scots Fusiliers, in 1959, to form the Royal Highland Fusiliers. The elephant insignia was awarded to the 74th Highlanders (later 2nd Battalion HLI) for their epic stand at the Battle of Assaye, in India, in 1803.

Maryhill Barracks, opened in 1876, superceded infantry barracks in Gallowgate where, according to Lord Provost Peter Clouston, 'the men were exposed to temptation of no ordinary character by coming into contact with the most dissolute and profligate portion of the population'.

The **Castle Vaults**

5 Maryhill Road, G20
0141 332 4522

A friendly no-frills Maryhill local, opened in 1898. The original owners were brothers George and John MacLachlan. The MacLachlans were pioneers of 'tied houses', whereby pubs were bought and used as outlets for a firm's own products – the MacLachlans owned the Castle Brewery at Maryhill and the Auchentoshan Distillery at Duntocher and sold 'Castle Brand' ales and stouts and 'Five Castle', 'Iona' and 'Auchentoshan' whiskies. The nerve centre of their operations was Castle Chambers in West Regent Street. In the early 1900s, the brothers ran 'model' pubs, refusing to sell 'kill-the-carter' (raw, fiery whisky) and loudly proclaiming that they would never serve drink to a

policeman in uniform (which makes you wonder what other pub owners got up to). Their empire was ultimately absorbed by J&R Tennent. While the interior of The Castle Vaults has been modernised, the original frontage remains and still carries the castle trademark of the MacLachlans, whose motto was 'Fortis et Fidus'.

The Crow Tavern

118 Kirkintilloch Road, G64
0141 762 3131

Though Bishopbriggs escaped annexation by Glasgow, the village became a dormitory surburb of the city where typical interwar bungalows sold for as little as £450. The present hostelry was formerly a simple vernacular wayside inn. It was remodelled in 1902 by a young Glasgow architect, Alexander McDonald, who gave the old howff a more sophisticated, sub-art nouveau character. While most of the original decor has gone, the present pub,with upstairs and downstairs bars, is very

attractive, with a traditional island bar at street level. Food served 12-3 in both bars. Live entertainment Fri-Sat.

Harvey's

1482 Maryhill Road, G20
0141 945 3286

A well-patronised local, situated in a typical 'Glasgow Style' tenement of the early

1900s, opposite the old Maryhill Burgh Hall. The art nouveau frontage survives, minus the engraved glass. Similarly, the island bar and gantry have gone. The elaborate ceiling remains.

In the late 18th century, with the Forth and Clyde canal passing through their Gairbraid estate, Mary Graham (née Hill) and her husband Robert profited from the new mode of transport by feuing part of the estate as an industrial village, 'in all time coming to be called Maryhill'. By 1850, the population had risen to around 3,000. When the burgh of Maryhill was absorbed into Glasgow, in 1891, it was a community of factories, workshops and tenements. In 1829, when a Men's Temperance Society was formed in Maryhill village, there was a tavern for every 59 residents.

The **Lee**

100 St James Road, G4
0141 564 1973

Modern (1990s) free house consisting of lounge and public bar, opposite Strathclyde University's Curran Library and a short walk from the area's cultural amenities – St Mungo Museum of Religious Life and Art, Provand's Lordship and Glasgow Cathedral. Good range of pub meals and snacks, including children's menu, served Mon-Sat until 6.30; Sunday until 4.30. Live music on Sunday evenings. Car park. The clientele here is mainly local, consisting of Townhead folk, though, thanks to comprehensive development in the 1960s and 70s, the area is only a shadow

of its former bustling self. Townhead's last historic pub, The Royal Bar, Glebe Street, a real ale oasis with antique beer fonts, bit the dust about a decade ago.

The drinking fountain which stands outside this pub was erected in 1908 by William Annan, a local spirit merchant. It originally stood at the Castle Street end of Stirling Road. Annan, who appears to have been rather

dotty, liked to be known as 'the Provost of Port Dundas'. No doubt the natives kept up the harmless pretence (as long as 'the Provost' was paying for the drinks).

A short stroll from here in the northerly direction of the notorious Townhead interchange will take you to Martyrs Public School, built by Charles Rennie Mackintosh in 1895-98. Some schools erected under the provisions of the 1872 Education (Scotland) Act were grim and forbidding. Mackintosh showed that the stringent financial limitations of Victorian School Boards could be overcome by the imagination and humanity of a great architect.

The **Politician**

1350 Maryhill Road, G20
0141 576 0180

Popular bar/lounge decorated with interesting photographs of Forth and Clyde Canal scenes. Basic pub menu available. Karaoke Fri nights, Disco Sats.

Quin's

130 Kirkintilloch Road, G64

Mrs Agnes Quin's pub, at 726 Springburn Road, no longer exists, but Quin's well-run Edwardian bar in Bishop-briggs is still going strong. Period features include pillars with ornate capitals and an elegant gantry with pediment and clock.

The name Bishopbriggs is thought to link the mediaeval village with the bishops of Glasgow, who received teinds from its riggs (strips of arable ground).

The Royalty Alehouse

144 Maryhill Road, G20
0141 332 1321

In the early 1990s, this was The Royalty Bar, a long-established Maryhill local. Now refurbished in Victorian vernacular fashion, the public bar here has a bare wood floor, matchboard dado, lincrusta-style wallpaper, and coffered ceiling. Inexpensive snacks and meals served all day. Karaoke evenings and live music sessions.

Viking Bar

1190 Maryhill Road, G2
0141 946 6195

Though Vikings from Scandinavia frequently came to Scotland to pillage and/or socialise, there's no evidence that they ever got as far as Maryhill Road. Since the 1960s, however, there has been a trend in the direction of fanciful pub names and associations. This is a basic Maryhill lounge bar, with strong local affiliations.

INDEX

INDEX